Group Medical Appointments

Group medical appointments (GMAs) are customized, extended medical appointments with a patient's own doctor and a behavioral health professional. Patients served best by GMAs are those with chronic conditions who require extensive monitoring, support, and follow up. *Group Medical Appointments* offers medical group managers, private practice clinicians, nurse executives, and behavioral health professionals vital information for increasing patients' and health professionals' satisfaction and level of care.

This must-have resource details the plethora of possibilities afforded by group medical appointments, including a wider range of support, greater focus on the individual's care, as well as more efficient, cost-effective treatment—essentially a "how to" book for Group or Shared Medical appointments. It includes the definition, how to use groups and all of the tools and scripts needed for a successful start-up. These groups have been found to address access issues in a practice and often leverage the providers' productivity by 200% during the same time as individual appointments. They have been found to increase positive outcomes of chronic disease which is covered in the book. They are first and foremost a medical appointment by providing support, education and are found to be therapeutic by participants.

Group Medical Appointments

A Step-by-Step Guide for Health Professionals

DeeAnn Schmucker

Routledge
Taylor & Francis Group
A PRODUCTIVITY PRESS BOOK

Designed cover image: Shutterstock

First published 2026
by Routledge
605 Third Avenue, New York, NY 10158

and by Routledge
4 Park Square, Milton Park, Abingdon, Oxon, OX14 4RN

Routledge is an imprint of the Taylor & Francis Group, an informa business

ISBN: 978-1-041-14243-0 (hbk)
ISBN: 978-1-041-14242-3 (pbk)
ISBN: 978-1-003-67352-1 (ebk)

DOI: 10.4324/9781003673521

Typeset in Garamond
by Deanta Global Publishing Services, Chennai, India

This book is dedicated to my family

Contents

Acknowledgments

I wish to acknowledge and thank John Scott, MD, Professor at the University of Colorado, and Marlene McKenzie, RN, Group Medical Appointment Consultant, for their invaluable contributions to the development of GMAs. Your experience, data, and patient stories about GMAs has added depth and increased the quality of this tool. I also wish to thank Del Gautsche, MSW, Group Medical Appointment Consultant, Strategies for Clinical Innovation, for his recent contributions to group medical appointments; you recognize the contribution this tool makes to medicine and patients. Your energy and creativity will further develop group medical appointments.

I would like to also acknowledge and thank the following medical practices and medical partners for being part of the continued advancement of GMAs through your willingness to be innovative, imaginative, and creative. I have learned and passed on much from what we have accomplished together.

Sutter Medical Foundation, Sacramento, California.

Sutter Medical Group, Sacramento, California.

Sutter West Medical Group, Davis, California.

Sutter Independent Physicians, Sacramento, California.

Sansum Medical Foundation, Santa Barbara, California.

Veteran's Administration Medical Center, Reno, Nevada.

Veteran's Administration Medical Center, Portland, Oregon.

Malcolm Grow USAF Medical Center, Andrews Air Force Base, Maryland.

Beal Air Force Medical Center, Beal Air Force Base, California.

David Grant Medical Center, Travis Air Force Base, California.

Walter Reed Army Medical Center, Washington, D.C.

Arroyo Secco Medical Group, Pasadena, California.

Valley Medical Group, Inc., Bakersfield, California.

Partnership Health Plan of California.

Pfizer Pharmaceuticals Harbor UCLA Medical Group, Torrance, California.

Foreword

In 1776, the life expectancy in the United States was 35 years, the average age of the population was 16 years, and physicians, with no technology and few effective drugs, saw patients in one-on-one appointments for acute medical problems.

Two hundred and thirty years later, the fastest-growing segment of the population is over 80 years of age. Diagnostic and therapeutic technology, along with advances in pharmacotherapy have, by necessity, resulted in physician specialists and subspecialists. Acute illness, for many physicians, has become a break in a day otherwise devoted to the management of chronic diseases. Informed patients expect, and the law demands, that all options for diagnosis and treatment be thoroughly discussed, and physicians are still seeing patients in one-on-one appointments.

The Institute of Medicine notes that there is a "quality chasm" between the state of medical knowledge and the care actually delivered to patients. Pundits ponder but the answer seems obvious particularly to primary care physicians. There is not enough time to do what we know we should do. All resources, nurses, nurse practitioners, physician assistants, and institutions are stretched to their limits and all are still seeing patients one-on-one.

We need an alternative delivery system. This book discusses one of those alternatives: group medical appointments. A key facet of this system is that it taps into a huge well of resources for management of chronic illness, the patients themselves. Patients collectively have vast experience and great wisdom in living with multiple chronic medical conditions. Creating an environment where many of the coping issues, compliance issues, education, and support can be addressed by the patients themselves is far more efficient and, accumulating data suggests, more effective than one-on-one time with physicians or other caregivers.

Many people believe that the financial structure of the current medical system is unsustainable and that fees-for-service medicine is antithetical to population management. If those people are correct, the next generation of physicians will need new tools for a new system in order to manage a population with multiple chronic illnesses in an efficient and cost-effective manner. Psychiatry has been doing it for 70 years. It is time for the rest of us to get on board.

John Scott, MD

Preface

This is the second edition of this book. Since the first writing, very little has changed regarding Group Medical Appointments, especially in terms of the history, the setups, potential pitfalls, and everything this book originally covered. What has changed is telehealth. Groups are now being conducted virtually with great success. As the landscape of healthcare changes, including fewer providers and limited rural access, doing groups virtually can significantly improve access to care. The potential for this tool remains untapped. Its adaptability gives us a tool to help navigate an uncertain future in healthcare. I encourage my readers to continue my work in leaning into this potential.

> *All truth passes through three stages. First, it is ridiculed. Second, it is violently opposed. Third, it is accepted as being self-evident.*
>
> **Arthur Schopenhauer (1788–1860)**

I first encountered Group Medical Appointments (GMAs) in 1999 and quickly realized that they could transform the way we treat chronic illness. Since that time, I have been working with health care organizations and private practices to develop their GMAs. I now believe that this powerful new paradigm can change the way we practice medicine and take the relationship between physicians and patients to a whole new level of satisfaction and healing.

When I realized the enormous possibilities that GMAs offered to patients with chronic diseases, I wanted to spread the word. In 1999, I began at Sutter Medical Foundation in Sacramento, managing their pilot program for GMAs. At Sutter, most of the GMAs we developed had the primary care physician as the common factor. We started with three Primary Care GMAs and one Rheumatology group. We learned as we went along, by constantly innovating and experimenting with the model. Our start-up was funded by a pharmaceutical company. This helped pay for salaries and consultation during the initial three-month pilot phase.

After six months, GMAs were expanded to include 15 new groups in the Sacramento region, mostly for primary care patients but also for Podiatry, Endocrinology and Women's Health, Rheumatology, OB/GYN (prenatal, postpartum, and perimenopause/menopause), Internal Medicine, Neurology, and Urology. More groups came later and new groups are continuing to be developed at Sutter.

Our goal was to improve both patient and physician satisfaction and to increase access to care. GMAs did all of those things: Our patients saw their physicians more frequently, felt better, lowered their use of medications, improved their labs, and went back to work after being on disability. They became true partners in their own care.

Physicians loved the groups. They could finally practice the medicine that was in their hearts, giving each patient more attention and a wider range of treatment and support without compromising financial or insurance requirements, or extending their hours. They could actually spend less time, accomplish more healing, and increase reimbursements per hour.

As time went on, we quickly began to develop GMAs based on the identification of specific issues the provider and staff wanted to address. So the groups started from the ground up with queries identifying the specific pressing needs and the best utilization of the current resources available to that provider and the situation. Groups continue to spread throughout Sutter Health combining some elements from the cooperative health care clinic (CHCC) model, some from the drop-in medical care (DIGMA) model, and many additional elements, which come into being through teamwork and creative problem-solving of the Sutter GMA department, the providers, and staff. These models will be described in more detail further on in the book.

I started groups for Sutter Medical Foundation throughout the Sacramento/Sierra Region, which includes small mountain towns, rural areas, university communities as well as the metro area of Sacramento. Sutter Medical Foundation continues utilizing GMAs and expands their use throughout the system. While working at Sutter, I have also had my own consulting practice. This has allowed for many more innovations to be spread across the country as I can take what I learn from each organization and share it.

My professional focus for more than 20 years has been chronic disease management. I have worked in both inpatient and outpatient settings that included extended care, dialysis, neonatal intensive care, home care, health education and program development for diabetes, chronic pain, asthma, depression, and healthy aging.

These patients face special challenges, as do people with other chronic conditions such as arthritis, high blood pressure, cancer, high cholesterol, and hypertension. Their bodies simply don't work the way they used to work or the way that other people's bodies work. They often feel helpless and out of control. This sense of hopelessness, that nothing will help, can make their symptoms even worse.

In order to live full lives, patients frequently need to change their ideas about what they can do, and how they can do it. They almost always need to make lifestyle or behavioral changes, and that takes time and attention. We can't just give these people a pill or a procedure and send them on their way. Patients need ongoing follow-up and attention that is not just physical, but also psychological, emotional, social, and sometimes even spiritual. They are best served in an environment that addresses a wide range of issues, in depth and as needed.

GMAs give patients exactly that environment. They get more attention and a wider range of support than they could get from individual appointments with one primary care physician. Patients can be seen as often as necessary. They can partner with a team of health professionals that may include psychologists, health educators, nurses, social workers, and other health professionals. They can make choices about their lives, develop their own action plans, and have greater control over the experience of their illness.

Chronic illness also creates an enormous opportunity for personal growth—and GMAs support this process as well. Patients, whose lives have been dramatically altered, are forced to reexamine their values and priorities. They start to focus inward and build a rich inner life based on what is truly important to them. I have been using personal growth and self-help principles with chronically ill patients since 1993, and GMAs are the perfect place to maximize this kind of inquiry. The inclusion of Group Medical Appointment Facilitators in the appointment and the group support that is present in GMAs make them excellent venues for patients to master skills, principles, and tools for personal growth.

Patients with chronic diseases may still be limited physically, but GMAs can help them gain control over their *responses* to their conditions. They become empowered. They begin to pick up the reins of their lives, and to grow in ways that may not have been possible without the GMA.

GMAs are a practice management tool that brings tremendous value and relief to physicians, staff, and patients alike. They are an outlet for everyone's creativity and a way to provide more and better support and education. They deliver more efficient, cost-effective treatment and create more satisfaction for everyone involved.

This book has been written for people who have never heard of GMAs, for those who are just starting up their programs, and for those who have programs already underway. It's important to share all that I have learned so that you won't have to waste time and resources making the same mistakes that I made when

I first started. My goal is for this book to help you proceed quickly and directly to the benefits of GMAs.

To that end, I have included the rationale for GMAs, snapshots of various types of GMAs, and the benefits that accrue both to patients and to physicians, plus a step-by-step guide for setting up GMAs in your practice.

> You are invited to use this extraordinary new tool to increase everybody's satisfaction, save time and money, and make possible a greater range of physical and psychological healing—and also to have more fun!

DeeAnn Schmucker MSW, LCSW

About the Author

DeeAnn K. Schmucker, MSW, LCSW, graduated from Hesston College in Hesston, Kansas. She received a bachelor's degree in social work from Bowling Green State University, U.S.A. and completed a Master of Social Work Degree, specializing in health care, at the University of Illinois, Urbana-Champaign, U.S.A. Throughout her career, DeeAnn has created focused therapies for a wide range of populations. She has worked in long-term care facilities, neonatal intensive care units, inpatient acute and rehabilitation hospitals, and a variety of outpatient settings.

Whatever the setting or situation, DeeAnn is always nudging others to take action that will improve the quality of their lives. As a health educator, she implemented a walking club and a book club for seniors to maintain their physical and mental abilities and to develop and foster supportive relationships. She became a trusted confidante and mentor, encouraging each participant one step farther today than yesterday or one question deeper into the theme of a novel. The interest and trust shown allowed participants to share aspects of themselves and stories that are part of their life history and that they never had the opportunity to share with others before. As a result, healing occurred, and each person's health was taken to a new level.

DeeAnn has written a variety of health education courses covering the topics of mental health and retirement, stress management, healthy lifestyle choices for seniors, and staff training manuals about sensitivity training for senior citizen patients. Collaborating with Kate Lorig, RN, DrPH, Stanford University School of Medicine Professor, and Director, Patient Education Research Center, DeeAnn co-developed a course for patients with chronic pain. By helping these patients understand the pain cycle, the patients could see behaviors that contributed to their pain and make modifications in those behaviors. Recently, DeeAnn has broadened her study of pain learning from John E. Leonard, PhD, and his Neurobehavioral Programs, another tool to help patients turn off their pain.

Establishing a group medical appointment program gave DeeAnn an ideal setting and opportunity to use these, as well as all of her other skills to enhance the patient's and physician's experience of health care. As a facilitator, she created an environment for patients and physicians to learn not only from her, but also from each other. DeeAnn is quick, however, to say that she is the one who learned the most. With the added support of a group, patients in group medical appointments made changes in weeks that they had not been able to make in years. Physicians experienced joy in practicing medicine again; some physicians said group medical appointments kept them from leaving medicine.

These experiences made DeeAnn an enthusiastic proponent of this tool. As a consultant and group medical appointment champion, she skillfully and with the wisdom of years of experience speaks directly to the concerns of skeptics. Ironically, these very skeptics are the ones who often end up being the first to start a group medical appointment in their organization. They begin to see that there is another way to provide health care where patients are partners in addressing their health and that of the other group members. This makes the physician's job easier.

Creating opportunities for patients to be partners in their health care is a lifelong pursuit for DeeAnn. She continues to learn something new from each interaction she has, whether it is nudging a patient, challenging a physician, or collaborating with another pioneer to develop even more strategies for clinical innovation.

DeeAnn makes her home with her husband Darrel; two children, Eric and Kaitlin; and toy fox terrier, Rosie, in northern California. She balances her professional work with good friendships, daily walks along the American River, singing, avid reading, and as much fun and laughter as others are able to tolerate.

THE RIGHT DIRECTION

I

Part I offers an overview of group medical appointments, with a focus on showing their potential to solve some of the most acute problems in health care today, illustrating how they can be used in a variety of circumstances, and describing the many ways they benefit both patients and physicians.

DOI: 10.4324/9781003673521-1

Chapter 1

The Potential of Group Medical Appointments

We all agree that your theory is crazy, but is it crazy enough?

Niels Bohr (1885–1962)

Group medical appointments (GMAs) are an elegant, efficient, cost-effective, and life-affirming solution to serious challenges that both physicians and patients face under our current health care system—challenges that will become more acute as Baby Boomers age.

GMAs give patients a wide spectrum of healing and support that is simply not possible in traditional individual appointments. They allow physicians to see at least twice as many patients in the same amount of time using existing resources. They deepen and broaden the quality of care for all patients, but they are particularly useful in treating patients with chronic conditions. This population is growing rapidly and will flood the health care system over the next 30 years.

Physicians who make the evolutionary step to GMAs usually become their most enthusiastic advocates. These physicians report that they can finally practice the kind of caring, holistic medicine that inspired them to become doctors in the first place. They can treat the whole person and provide solutions that truly enhance the quality of people's lives. The bonus is that in addition, physicians realize substantial savings in time, energy, and money.

DOI: 10.4324/9781003673521-2

This book is written for physicians, administrators, and managers of medical practices and other healthcare organizations. It describes the enormous potential of GMAs to

- Increase access.
- Improve outcomes.
- Promote a supportive healing environment that places patients at the center of a health care team that treats the entire person.
- Create a partnership between patients and physicians in which patients play an active role in their own healing and have support in making lifestyle changes that enrich their lives.
- Help medical practices effectively treat more patients in less time, with less stress, using existing resources.
- Put enjoyment and creativity back into medicine for both physicians and patients.

Part I describes a brief history of GMAs and how GMAs provide solutions to some of the most pressing problems in health care today. It illustrates how they work, why they work, the many ways that they can be used, and the benefits they bring to patients, physicians, practices, and medical organizations.

Part II is a step-by-step guide to setting up GMAs in your practice. This guide shows you how to market and enroll patients into GMAs and how to organize them so that they run efficiently and bring greater satisfaction to physicians, staffs, and patients. It is filled with principles, practices, tips, and tools to help people tailor GMAs to their individual situations and make them work in a variety of circumstances.

Where Did This Concept Come from?

A Brief Look at the History of GMAs

History of Medicine

> *I have a headache . . .*
> *2000 BC: Eat this root.*
> *AD 1000: That root is infected, say this prayer.*
> *AD 1850: That prayer is superstition, drink this potion.*
> *AD 1940: That potion is snake oil, swallow this pill.*
> *AD 1985: That pill is ineffective, take this antibiotic.*
> *AD 2000: That antibiotic is artificial, eat this root.*
>
> **Aha! Jokes, http://www.AhaJokes.com/**

GMAs have been part of medicine for an undeterminable amount of time. Before individual appointments with a physician in an office existed, there were GMAs. We all remember hearing stories and seeing movies of how physicians used to visit patients in their homes and sit by their bedside with other family members providing care. At that time, comfort and problem-solving were often the only assistance that the physician could provide, as the powerful drugs and surgical procedures that we have today were not in existence. Hospitals were designed to have wards, not the private or semi-private rooms that we have today. Information about the patients in the ward was shared in front of everyone, and it was not uncommon for other patients to make comments. Even in the semi-private rooms that we often have today, the roommate or the roommate's family gives information to the physician about the patient. A physician told me a story that illustrated this point well: The physician went into the hospital room to check on his patient, and he asked the patient how he slept. The patient complained that he did not get a wink of sleep that entire night. The roommate interrupted and said, "I know you slept because your snoring kept me awake."

Care delivered in a group found a solid beginning in the treatment of large numbers of soldiers who were returning from World War II. The military has a long history of using GMAs as new recruits were often given physicals all together in the same room. Although the current group appointments for physicals are designed also to provide the patient with information and lifestyle change support, both types of physicals accomplish better use of time and resources.

Mental health long ago began group appointments for the treatment of a variety of conditions as they recognized that the group itself was therapeutic and provided an additional tool or treatment modality for clients. Self-help groups sprang up in the 1970s to assist people in dealing with specific issues. These groups are not traditionally led by a professional, but group members themselves appoint or volunteer to lead the group. Alcoholics Anonymous and Weight Watchers are excellent examples of successful self-help groups.

I have the opportunity to work with a variety of medical groups and physicians in private practice and am amazed to hear the stories of their own experimentation with GMAs. Often they have had different types of groups for many years, but had not written about them or studied them. Pioneers are encouraged to step forward with their experiences to enrich all of us as we look at this treatment model.

Innovators Who Have Written and Studied GMAs

Joseph Hersey Pratt (1872–1956)

The first to use and write about GMAs was Joseph H. Pratt, an internist at Massachusetts General Hospital in Boston. The year was 1905, and Dr Pratt began these groups by offering general care instruction groups for newly discharged tuberculosis patients. Among other items explained to the patients during the group, the necessity of hygienic instruction was taught, with Dr Pratt persuading them to be submissive to his will.

Although antibiotics have totally transformed how we treat tuberculosis patients today, at that time, treatment included dealing with what we now call the psychosocial aspects of the disease, as there were many psychosomatic conditions and emotional factors of chronic and recurrent tuberculosis. As Dr Pratt continued his development of these groups, he noticed the impact of the group experience on the emotional status of the patients who attended. Seven years after he began working with tuberculosis patients in groups, Dr Pratt adapted the model for treatment of patients with chronic psychosomatic conditions. These groups were known as the Thought Control Class at the Boston Dispensary. Several other physicians followed his lead in treating physical conditions in a group setting. Later, in the 1920s and 1930s, Dr Pratt introduced the concept to psychiatric patients, where he placed more emphasis on emotions and their effect on the disease process than on the disease itself.

Other early innovators include Paul Schilder and Louis Wender, who in the 1930s applied the group concepts to provide therapy for prison inmates and discharged mental patients. During the 1930s, this model was found to be very useful in the treatment of children and adolescents.

John Scott, MD, and Marlene McKenzie, RN

Dr John Scott, a Kaiser Permanente, Colorado, internist and geriatrician, developed the Cooperative Health Care Clinic Model in 1991. His interest was to provide quality health care to senior members and to deliver the care in an effective and efficient manner that would benefit both providers and patients. His desire grew from a sense a frustration that his patients were not receiving the kind of care they needed in a typical 15-minute office visit. Dr Scott assembled a team of colleagues, including physicians, nurses, administrators, and researchers. In designing a new way to deliver the care, the team kept in mind this motto: "What would my mother want?" The team recognized the value of providing patients with regular ongoing access to their primary care physician and health care team, establishing an environment for sharing educational information and peer support. The result of the collaborative endeavor was the Cooperative Health Care Clinic (CHCC). This group visit model brings together 15 to 20 patients of the practicing physician for a 2.5-hour monthly group visit. The same patients meet together in a conference room with their physician and members of the health care team. The primary purpose of this group visit is to provide health care along with education and social support. The details of this model are described in depth in Chapter 2.

Three randomized controlled studies have been conducted at Kaiser Permanente, Colorado, comparing the group visit model to usual care. All demonstrate the benefits of offering care in a group model. Results are shared in depth in Chapter 2.

Group visits have become a standard model of practice for numerous physicians at Kaiser Permanente. Groups are not only offered for seniors, but also for numerous patient populations, such as those with fibromyalgia, diabetes, asthma, hypertension, and women's health concerns and those needing preoperative education and evaluation, radiation oncology consults, and prenatal and well-baby checkups.

Marlene McKenzie, RN, MN, contributor to this book, coordinated the second research study. In addition to her research activities, she trained and mentored all physicians and nurses within the Colorado region in launching CHCC groups and provided consultative support and leadership to specialty areas launching groups.

Ed Noffsinger, PhD

Ed Noffsinger, PhD, a health psychologist from Kaiser Permanente, San Jose Medical Center, developed the Drop In Group Medical Appointment (DIGMA) in 1996. Through his work with primary care and specialty care, he identified that physicians were struggling with deteriorating access, substantially increased workloads, growing patient demands and expectations, morale issues, and increasingly large patient loads. A tool was needed that would work equally in primary and specialty care to enable physicians to see dramatically more patients in the same amount of time. This would need to be done in a way that improved access, increased service and quality, and improved satisfaction for both physicians and patients alike. Out of these desires, the DIGMA model was developed.

The needs assessment Ed conducted came up with three categories of needs: timely access, patient satisfaction, and physician satisfaction. Ed also had his own health crisis and experienced personal frustration at connecting with his physician over the phone, feeling as if appointments were difficult to get and that he often felt rushed. Also, a number of physicians at this Kaiser were behind in their health maintenance for a significant number of their patients. It was those patients who first filled the first groups. From those needs, the DIGMA model was created.

The DIGMA model differs from the CHCC model in that it does not focus on specific patient populations, as does the CHCC model, but rather on the physician's entire patient panel. Another difference is that the group is co-facilitated with preferably a mental health professional or behaviorist, as called by Dr Noffsinger. The inclusion of a behaviorist increases the physicians' ability to see more patients in the given time and to complete the paperwork by the end of the group. The behaviorist starts the groups and then manages the time and patients to make sure that everyone gets ample time and that no one monopolizes the group. This group also differs because although patients are encouraged to call and schedule a group appointment, dropping in at the beginning of the group is also a way to participate. Dr Noffsinger also often recommends that the group be attended by someone who can do the chart note for the physician and the coding for billing and by a designated scheduler to keep the census up in the DIGMA appointments (Noffsinger, 1999c).

Dr Noffsinger developed four different types of DIGMA groups. The first is the Heterogeneous Model, in which patients may come for a large variety of reasons and conditions. The Homogeneous Model is one in which patients will be scheduled by having a similar disease state, and the Mixed Model is a combination of the Heterogeneous and Homogeneous Models. The fourth group type developed by Dr Noffsinger is called the Physical Model. People who come in for this model are initially taken to an exam room for the physical portion of the exam. They then dress and go to the group room with other patients where the physician then has the discussion with the entire group.

The DIGMA model is not discussed in further detail in this book using the term DIGMA. Some of the GMA models that will be discussed contain many of the elements of the DIGMA model.

DeeAnn Schmucker, LCSW, LICSW

In 1999 I started working with Group Medical Appointments, or Shared Medical Appointments, spring boarding off the work of my predecessors. The organization that I was working with at the time and I were the first to use group appointments in a mixed fee for service and capitated environment. This required identifying appropriate billing codes to bill insurance as opposed to the cost-saving environment of Kaiser. Much work went into assessing the legality of how to bill and how to be HIPAA compliant. I also greatly expanded the various types of group appointments and ways to utilize this tool. All of the above is addressed in greater detail later in this book.

I quickly realized that while group appointments provide medical treatment, they are also therapeutic and educational. Surprisingly, the group provides a synergy and connectedness among its participants that really amplifies the positive experience. I also realized that we as medical professionals can quickly make group appointments complicated, and we reduce the efficacy of them with our "good intentions." We can make them more work than they need to be. Sometimes this looks like making group appointments into too much of class. I have learned that presenting on a topic for 3–5 minutes, giving concise, user-friendly information goes much further as it allows time for the synergy and connectedness of participating in a group to occur. Make no mistake, classes and education are a valuable tool. However, too much time spent on education can get in the way of the dynamic healing that takes place when patients are able to interact fully with others in the group. Through this experience, I recognize that we as medical professionals are often more comfortable with teaching and don't always know how to facilitate a healing experience, especially in groups. This led me to develop a facilitator training program to help the medical professionals learn how to facilitate and use the group to provide education and support treatment options. It's this aspect that makes the group therapeutic and promotes better, longer-lasting lifestyle changes and creates more individual resiliency in the management of chronic conditions.

I also have innovated using group appointments as part of larger disease management programs that include classes, integrative medicine, mental health, and other pertinent treatments and allied professionals. In these settings, the group is again where the patient sees the physician or provider and then can share their experience with other areas of the program with other patients in the group.

I have always dreamed of group appointment being done via telehealth, and now some organizations are using the very model with success. I believe that my work and the work of my predecessors just scratched the surface of this tool and I look forward to seeing how others may advance group medical appointments.

Why GMAs? The Next Evolutionary Step

GMAs are an idea whose time has come. They were created specifically to address the current needs of both physicians and patients—needs that have evolved beyond the capacity of our health care system as it exists today. These needs grew out of critical shifts over the past few decades in how medicine is practiced, in the relationship between doctor and patient, in the number of patients who must be treated, and in the nature of their conditions.

Critical Shifts

> *The significant problems we face cannot be solved at the same level of thinking we were at when we created them.*
>
> **Albert Einstein (1879–1955)**

It is natural to see shifts in how medicine is practiced over the years, and it is natural to see shifts in the needs of the populations it serves. In an ideal world, the shifts in how health care is delivered match the shifting needs of patients. In the past few decades, however, our capacity to deliver what patients need has become severely impaired. This short history of the past 80 to 100 years shows how and why.

Until the advent of antibiotics, patients were generally treated in a supportive home environment. Healing often included home remedies and traditions passed down through families to maintain the health and cure the sick in that family. Physicians came to the house, usually because the patient had an infection of some kind, and did their best to cure it. Family members were usually involved, and health care was a hands-on team effort that involved empowerment of the patient and family, problem-solving, and support as valuable tools in the treatment of the patient.

Antibiotics made curing these infections a matter of writing prescriptions, and vaccinations helped control or eliminate many serious diseases. Medicine became largely about pharmaceuticals, with the physician moving away from the home to the office and providing the vaccines, or prescriptions, that were the key to health and longer life. The practice of medicine became less "hands on." In fact, it became almost entirely "hands off." As medicine now was more about curing the condition with pharmaceuticals, physicians took primary control of the treatment, creating a paternalistic model of care. The 1970s brought new pharmaceuticals, surgeries, and diagnostic tools that extended life dramatically. Open heart surgeries, bypasses, and powerful new medications made cardiovascular diseases survivable and increased life expectancy for people with various types of cancer. Physicians became master mechanics of the body, matching the procedure or drug to the disease, and moved even further away from the emotional and psychological sides of healing. Specialized training in related organ or body systems became a major part of physician training, as every medical student also needed to choose a specialization in order to practice medicine. Medical professionals began to see patients as "disease states" and moved away from looking at and treating the entire person. Patients became accustomed to seeing specialists and measuring the quality of care based on their access to specialty services. Many patients erroneously felt a loss of control with the need for an authorization in order to see a specialist.

As life spans increased and the population grew and aged, more people began living with such chronic diseases as arthritis, diabetes, depression, chronic pain, cancer, high cholesterol, asthma, and hypertension. The surgeries, procedures, and pharmaceuticals that had extended life did not always, by themselves, have a significant impact on these chronic diseases. All of these conditions had psychological components, and almost all of them required changes in lifestyle and behavior—often, big changes.

"Hands Off" to "Hands On"

We have found that when patients can make these lifestyle changes, they are better able to manage their diseases and can significantly improve the quality of their lives. Making the changes, however, usually requires a holistic approach, emotional support, information, problem-solving, and ongoing attention. Making lifestyle changes requires time, partnership with providers, and access to mental health, community, and social services that are rarely available under our current systems.

Managing these chronic diseases requires hands-on healing—by now, health care has become almost exclusively hands off. We are back to needing education, human interactions, partnering relationships, frequent visits, and a circle of support. The relationship between patient and physician has become paternalistic and often distant. Moreover, physicians are not always the best equipped for dealing with psychological and behavioral issues. *This is where most care begins and ends.* Thus, patients rarely get all of what they need.

Physicians try harder and harder to meet these needs, seeing many more patients than is realistic in the course of a day, but they usually come up short. They want to serve their patients but are handicapped by the constraints of organizational restrictions and/or insurance regulations, the fact that there are only 24 hours in a day, and the antiquated system of individual appointments. They, too, are frustrated. They are giving everything they have, and more, and still not getting the results they want.

Patients and physicians walk away from one another feeling frustrated. The current system is not working for anybody. Our needs have come full circle, but the way we deliver health care has not. We as health professionals have used the individual appointment to meet the vast majority of patient needs and have spent the better part of the last two decades trying to "fix" the individual appointment. Nothing is wrong with the individual appointment except when we try to use it as the only treatment modality for patients to see their providers. A gap exists between what patients need and what physicians can provide.

GMAs correct this condition and fill the gap. They offer both physicians and patients relief from the frustration and provide many ancillary benefits as well.

> *All human actions have one or more of these seven causes: chance, nature, compulsion, habit, reason, passion, and desire.*
>
> **Aristotle—Greek critic, philosopher, physicist, and zoologist (384–322 BC)**

New Challenges, New Needs

> *If you think you can do a thing or think you can't do a thing, you're right.*
>
> **Henry Ford—U.S. automobile industrialist (1863–1947)**

The new challenges that these critical shifts have created ask us to look outside of the box for solutions. Before we can do that, we need to see exactly what our current needs are. They include the following:

1. *Greater access for patients.* Many patients have difficulty gaining access to their physicians and spending "quality time" with them when they do get access. They want and need more time and more attention, but physicians are already stretched too thin. This need for more access is particularly pressing for patients with chronic illnesses, challenging psychosocial issues, and other conditions that involve adjusting medications or modifying behavior. These patients need to be seen by the physician frequently, and physicians simply do not have time for frequent follow-ups with every patient. Chronic conditions are best treated through a variety of avenues, and the treatment for each patient needs to be customized to deal with the patient's particular concerns. Physicians and patients need time to plan and experiment with medications and treatment options in order to find an effective plan for the patient. This need is exacerbated by the fact that chronic diseases are rising exponentially as the population ages.
2. *Treatment of the whole person—including emotional, behavioral, lifestyle, and psychosocial factors.* Patients with chronic diseases need a place to address the behavioral, psychological, and emotional components of their conditions, which are often outside the physician's range. Physicians are restricted by financial, legal, and organizational considerations—the rushed environment of conducting individual appointments every 10 to 15 minutes is simply not conducive to dealing with these personal and psychological issues.
3. *Ongoing support and education.* These same patients often need ongoing support and education. Their medications need to be adjusted. They need to be monitored to be sure that they are making required lifestyle changes, and they need to have their questions answered. Physicians do not have the time to provide this kind of support and education over and over in a series of 10- or 15-minute appointments.
4. *Partnership between physician and patient.* Patients want to be equals, and healing is most effective when they partner with physicians in their own

care. Often their attempts to put the relationship on a more equal and personal footing—usually by small talk and personal questions—only consume time that might otherwise be spent on their care. The less they get this equal relationship, the more they want it and the more they *try* to get it—even though the physician may be edging toward the door because he or she is already an hour behind schedule. This situation only produces more frustration for everyone.

5. *Greater satisfaction and less stress for physicians.* Doctors want to give patients what they need, but the way medicine is practiced today often does not allow them to do so. They run from one individual appointment to the next, doing everything they can, but knowing that it is not enough. They are exhausted at the end of the day, but they often do not have the satisfaction of knowing that they are providing the level of care their patients want and need. Physicians also experience increasing amounts of stress in trying to meet the Health Employer Data Information Set (HEDIS) requirements and demands from practice guidelines.
6. *Economic viability.* Physicians are under tremendous pressure to reduce the cost of care without compromising quality. These needs must be met in a way that allows health care delivery to remain viable and productive—using current resources wherever possible.

In the current medical environment, it is very difficult to address these many issues. We need a fundamental shift in how medicine is practiced, one that creates a new relationship between doctor and patient and that meets the challenges that both patients and physicians face today.

Patients' and physicians' problems under the current system are interconnected. Fortunately, so are the solutions.

The Elegant Solution

GMAs speak directly to these pressing needs. They improve both access and quality of care. They add the psychological and behavioral component in an effortless, seamless way. They provide for ongoing education and support. They let physicians and patients relate as human beings in a healing partnership that benefits them both. In this sense, GMAs represent the first real shift in the patient–physician relationship in the last 100 years. The result is improved visits, and each visit becomes more satisfying for both physician and patient.

What do GMAs actually look like? Chapter 2 gives full descriptions of several kinds of GMAs and shows how they are effective with various patient populations and practice settings. This preview is meant to give you a basic snapshot of GMAs. It is a place to start looking at what kind of GMA might work for you and to begin thinking about how to shape group appointments to best serve your practice.

An Example of a GMA

The GMA is first and foremost a medical appointment. It is not therapy, a support group, or a class—but it is therapeutic, supportive, and educational in ways that often exceed what physicians can offer in the limited time available during office visits.

The American Academy of Family Physicians defines GMAs this way:

> A shared medical appointment, also known as a group visit, is when multiple patients are seen as a group for follow-up or routine care. These visits are voluntary for patients and provide a secure but interactive setting in which patients have improved access to their physicians, the benefit of counseling with additional members of a health care team (for example, a behaviorist, nutritionist, or health educator), and can share experiences and advice with one another.

We have found that physicians can easily leverage the number of patients they see by 200% and can also increase the quality of care at the same time. Patients pay their usual co-payment, and doctors bill the insurance companies the same way they would for individual appointments.

A variety of ways is available for doing GMAs. The CHCC is one of the first GMAs researched and written about and is discussed in detail in Chapter 2.

Example of a GMA with a Facilitator

Patients arrive at the designated time for the GMA. They check in and make their co-payment and are ushered into the group room, which usually has chairs arranged in a semicircle (Figure 1.1). While the patients are arriving and getting settled, the nurse or medical assistant begins to take them to a private area to record their vital signs. The GMA may begin when two to three patients have their vital signs taken. The remaining vital signs can be taken while the group is in process. The physician sits next to the facilitator, who is usually a health professional. The facilitator works in concert with the doctor during the GMA. He or she helps to manage the group's energy and time and may bring to light underlying psychosocial issues, give advice, invite discussion, or suggest referrals for behavioral or psychosocial issues.

The facilitator opens the appointment by reviewing the purpose, format, procedures, confidentiality, and logistics of the GMA. Then the physician begins

Figure 1.1 Patients sitting in a group with an MA. *Photo courtesy of Tamara Scott © 2005.*

looking at the medical record and listening to what brought each person to the appointment. With the facilitator on one side and prescription pad, referral forms, and other tools on the other, the doctor addresses the health care needs of each patient. The facilitator makes sure that communication stays open and that the process keeps moving.

The atmosphere is caring, supportive, and compassionate—with a free exchange of information, ideas, and solutions among patients, physician, and facilitator. The give-and-take environment of GMAs allows information to flow more openly and for a longer period of time than is possible in brief individual consultations. Time and space are available to identify the psychosocial and emotional, as well as the physical, components of their conditions.

Group members empathize with one another and enjoy sharing knowledge and resources. The group is often full of laughter, tears, wisdom, and shared humanity. Family members, caregivers, and other significant people in the patients' lives are typically invited to attend, as they can be part of the healing. In the group setting, family members and caregivers can benefit from the interaction as well as learn how to support the patient better. We have found that when family members or caregivers participate in groups, we as medical professionals learn much more about how the patient manages and copes with his or her condition.

The facilitator opens the appointment by reviewing the purpose, format, procedures, confidentiality, and logistics of the GMA. Then the physician begins looking at the medical record and listening to what brought each person to the appointment. With the facilitator on one side and prescription pad, referral forms, and other tools on the other, the doctor addresses the health care needs of each patient. The facilitator makes sure that communication stays open and that the process keeps moving.

The atmosphere is caring, supportive, and compassionate—with a free exchange of information, ideas, and solutions among patients, physician, and facilitator. The give-and-take environment of GMAs allows information to flow more openly and for a longer period of time than is possible in brief individual consultations. Time and space are available to identify the psychosocial and emotional, as well as the physical, components of their conditions.

Group members empathize with one another and enjoy sharing knowledge and resources. The group is often full of laughter, tears, wisdom, and shared humanity. Family members, caregivers, and other significant people in the patients' lives are typically invited to attend, as they can be part of the healing. In the group setting, family members and caregivers can benefit from the interaction as well as learn how to support the patient better. We have found that when family members or caregivers participate in groups, we as medical professionals learn much more about how the patient manages and copes with his or her condition.

Groups can be formed for patients who have a specific disease or condition such as diabetes, depression, and chronic pain or specific surgeries such as vasectomies—they can be set up for people who have in common only that they are patients of one particular physician. These patients may have a variety of conditions and concerns. Individual medical exams are done during the group or as needed after the GMA, depending on the extent of the exam and patient preference.

Two (or More) for the Price of One: Benefits to Patients

First, let us look at how GMAs address patients' needs. Not only can patients be seen more quickly, more frequently, and for longer periods of time, but they also enjoy the attention of both the physician and the facilitator. They can get the needed medical treatment and also have the services of someone who speaks to their more holistic, emotional, behavioral, social, lifestyle, spiritual, and psychological needs. They are at the hub of a well-coordinated health care team that is focused on their well-being.

The group itself becomes part of the healing. Patients often say, "I don't feel so alone." They learn from one another, as well as from the physician and the facilitator. They challenge one another to succeed, give one another hope, and validate one another's successes. Contributing to others helps them feel better. We find joy when we make a contribution to someone else's life, and patients are no exception. Often, just making that contribution gives patients the courage and support to continue with their own struggles with their disease. Patients in GMAs have had great success making lifestyle changes such as diet, exercise, and quitting smoking with the support and resources available in the group.

They benefit not only from their own interactions with the physician, but also from observing other patients' treatment and hearing answers to other patients' questions and concerns. We often forget that many people are affected by many chronic diseases, whether they themselves have the disease or not, as patients often have family members and friends that deal with chronic diseases. Thus, they often take home information gained in the group and pass it on to a loved one.

Patients become better educated about health in general and about their own situation in particular so that they can become true partners in their own care. They also get immediate referrals to community and social services and to other medical or mental health professionals, as needed.

Having this kind of support improves their "perception of health." They feel more empowered to manage their disease and more in control. They expect more of themselves and often become more proactive about their own health. They are more inclined to try new solutions and to take better care of themselves. Some patients go back to work who had never expected to do so.

GMAs make the relationship between doctor and patient less paternalistic and more of a partnership. Patients are happier with their care. Even though their specific medical needs may only be addressed for 5 to 10 minutes, they have actually spent 60 to 120 minutes (depending on how long the group was scheduled) with their physician. This makes them feel as if they know the physician better. They are generally more satisfied, less needy, less inclined to become upset, less inclined to call the office repeatedly demanding attention, and more likely to follow the doctor's advice. Difficult patients, those who we dread seeing their names on the daily appointment list, behave better in GMAs. Groups are very dynamic and interesting, and the patients feel like they get special attention whether the group is focusing on them specifically or not.

Demographics

Age, race, and economic factors have not played a determining role in who attends the GMAs as chronic disease and the management of chronic disease are great equalizers. We have seen patients who are infants up through patients in their 90s with great results.

In the beginning, staff members were concerned about offering GMAs to working people, as they were afraid these patients would not be able to spend the time that the groups take. What we found was that in the first place a 90-minute group was generally about the same amount of time patients spent for their individual appointments, including waiting room time, exam room waiting time, and the appointment time with the provider. People who are working often discover that a GMA actually takes less time than an individual appointment. Working patients in a GMA can ask to be one of the first patients seen and then decide how long they want to stay. They like having more control of their time and how it is spent.

Another concern we had initially was having children in the GMAs, especially in family practice groups where adults are also being seen. This too has worked out very well. If the children are young, we generally address their needs in the early part of the group. If the children are old enough to understand the conversation, they tend to enjoy the groups. Teenagers especially enjoy the groups, as everyone is at the same level. They tend to take other adult patients' advice about smoking and other lifestyle behaviors to heart and make the necessary changes.

In terms of economic status, we have again had a good representation. We have had executives and welfare recipients in the same groups and have observed them interacting and helping each other. Not only is chronic disease a good equalizer, but relationship problems with children, parents, and spouses are prevalent at all levels of income.

The Mind–Body Connection

> *The doctor of the future will give no medication, but will interest his patients in the care of the human frame, diet and in the cause and prevention of disease.*
>
> **Thomas A. Edison**

One of the greatest benefits to patients is that GMAs treat the whole person—physical, emotional, psychological, and social. Because GMAs do effectively address the mind–body connection, they are exceptionally well suited to patients with chronic conditions. While the physician treats the physical side of the disease, a mental health facilitator can look at the patient's psychological context and help with emotional or lifestyle aspects of the condition. This frequently involves training patients in such areas as relaxation, coping skills, and education in self-management of chronic conditions.

Patients also have access to professional support and coaching from the facilitator in making lifestyle changes. Because they can be seen more frequently, these changes can be monitored and support given at closer intervals. In many instances, we find that patients' symptoms diminish, and they become more independent and report a better quality of life.

This matter-of-fact inclusion of psychological components also helps destigmatize such mental health issues as stress reactions, depression, and anxiety. Patients are often surprised to learn how common and treatable these conditions are. When they see these psychological components addressed regularly among other group members, a door opens for them to talk about their own symptoms. They can ask for help, instead of hiding their condition because they are ashamed or because "there isn't time." We also know that these issues often take more time for the provider to uncover. This is especially true for patients who have little experience with or knowledge of psychological issues and/or have many other conditions to treat.

Patients often accept psychological help more quickly and easily in the group. One woman had been depressed for some time, but had not realized what was wrong until she heard a man sitting next to her in the group talking about depression (Figure 1.2). Another patient heard the facilitator recommend therapy to a member of the group who had become her friend and realized that

Figure 1.2 Doctor speaking with patients. *Photo courtesy of Tamara Scott © 2005.*

such treatment "wasn't just for crazy people." Patients are more likely to move beyond their resistance to this kind of help when other patients share that they, too, had been reluctant but that the treatment had worked for them. Patients realize through these interactions that they are not alone and that what they are experiencing is often common among other patients. This greatly reduces the shame or the feeling that they have done something wrong, something to deserve this and instead helps patients view depression for what it is: a common medical condition that responds to treatment.

Satisfaction almost always improves among patients who attend GMAs—even when they have apprehension at first. One study at Reno Veterans Administration hospital compared patients' expectations of GMAs with their actual experience of the group. These patients actually had moderate to high expectations when they first completed the survey. A statistically significant number of them reported that their experience of the group was more positive than they had anticipated.

Leveraging at 200% to 300%: Benefits for Physicians

Physicians' time and energy are used far more efficiently and effectively in GMAs. They are reimbursed the same amount and in the same way as they would be if they raced from patient to patient 12 times. Instead, however, they spend a relaxed 90 minutes with the group and emerge energized for the rest of the day. They have time to be more caring, to be more creative, and to provide a broader range of healing. The providers I have worked with report that they learn more about their patients from one GMA than the 10 or 15 years that they have been seeing their patients in individual appointments. The benefit that most physicians mention is that the time they spend with patients is more relaxed, more intimate, and enhanced by the presence of the facilitator.

GMAs are also a breakthrough tool for managing costs. Thomas Atkins, MD, former chief medical officer for Sutter Medical Foundation, put it this way in a 2001 *Sacramento Bee* article:

> For years, we've been trying to make the system work better with all the money drained out. The cost pressures aren't going to go away. We have to think of new ways to deliver the care and groups are one way.

Another advantage that GMAs offer to physicians is that they only have to deliver information once, instead of 12 times. "I spend a lot of time with diabetic patients," explains Dan Fields, MD, at the Sutter Laguna Medical Group in Elk Grove, California (Figure 1.3).

Figure 1.3 Doctor lecturing to a group of patients. *Photo courtesy of Tamara Scott © 2005.*

> I hear the same stuff from these patients all day long, and it gets tiring having to repeat the information to them. It's great that I can get all the patients in one room and be able to talk to them at the same time.

GMAs make patients happy, and happy patients make a physician's life easier. "We first got interested in GMAs because we liked the idea of providing better care and also, very practically, we wanted to improve access," says Dr Daniel Berger, endocrinologist at Sansum Medical Foundation Clinic in Santa Barbara, California. "We have a very busy practice and it was difficult to see patients quickly without overbooking through lunch and at the end of the day."

The Sansum pilot, primarily for patients with diabetes, got under way in 2003. Dr Berger says,

> Our patients get a lot out of it. They're learning a lot of new things that they wouldn't get just in one-on-one appointments. We can make teaching points to the whole group. They feel freer in the group, and we have a behaviorist to help with their lifestyle issues. They're in a better mood than they are in the usual setting.

A New Partnership

Doctors and patients form a partnership in GMAs that is rare when patients are seen only in individual appointments. In the traditional setting, the relationship is defined as paternalistic. Everything is rushed, and patients and doctors often have different goals. From the moment the physician enters the room, the patient and physician compete with each other in how the time will be used. Patients want their questions answered and want to know how the physician will treat the rash or the other symptoms that the patient finds difficult to deal with. If the patient has one or more chronic conditions, the physician is asking questions and gathering data from the patient to determine how the disease is progressing and if the patient has something that could be considered life threatening or in need of immediate care. Often, symptoms that show disease progression or life-threatening situations are not so much of a bother to the patient. Patients feel dissatisfied, as they do not feel that enough emphasis was placed on the rash or non-urgent bothersome issues. They assume that their physician does not care or did not pay any attention to what they were saying. The model of care that we are most accustomed to views the patient as being a recipient of care, not a partner. Patients look to the physician to cure them or fix them. They feel dependent on the physician and depend on the physician to decide on the treatment plan. This dependency is fostered by having the patients sit in an exam room with their clothing removed. Patients are trying to get more time, more attention, and more equality. Doctors are trying to treat the disease and get on to the next appointment, for which they may be late.

GMAs bring relief by transforming this relationship into a more equal, cooperative partnership. Even patients who have been problematic, emotionally needy, anxious, or angry tend to relax when they can come to group regularly. The change is rewarding and positive.

Within this richer relationship and freed of the 10-minute time constraint, patients are often more willing to reveal information that can help in diagnosis and treatment.

"I get a lot more social history in groups," says Dr Berger.

> I thought they might not want to talk in the group about things they weren't proud of, things that were stressors in their lives. But just the opposite was true. Patients I'd been seeing for years brought things up in the group, like alcohol use, that I didn't know anything about. It hadn't come up in the one-on-one appointments. In group, they were far more comfortable talking about it. They are much more open with social history than in individual appointments.

GMAs allow physicians to work from a treatment model based on abundance, rather than on scarcity. There is enough time and enough energy for each patient to get what he or she needs and for both doctor and patient to feel good about the care that is provided. For example, physicians can bring newly diagnosed patients back at optimal intervals to check labs, medications, or lifestyle changes, rather than basing their decision on when to bring them back for a follow-up based on how long the patient can safely go without coming back.

Having Fun Again

My clients have seen physician satisfaction improve dramatically with GMAs. Unpublished studies at various medical groups that I have worked with have shown an increase in satisfaction. This occurs for many reasons. The workload is reduced. The schedule opens up, and doctors discover that they are actually having fun practicing medicine again—to mention just a few of the comments I have heard from physicians.

Dr Berger says,

> I look forward to GMA day every week. It's a change of pace, and we have fun. We do medicine, but it's on a lighter note. People say more about themselves, and they stick to their regimens better. I love the groups, and am going to create more of them.

Dr Mark Knoble, a family practice physician from Sutter Medical Group, Auburn, California, says that he rediscovered the joy he felt when he first started practicing. This is some of what he has to say about GMAs:

> Since beginning my groups in 2001, I have rediscovered the joy and satisfaction in providing healing care for my patients. What I see in group astounds me. Patients that I had been working with for years on an individual basis began to show improvement and stability. The group format helps them address, with the help of the mental health professional and the other group members, psychosocial or relational factors that may have been contributing to their illness or disease.
>
> The group also allows me the opportunity to re-invent health care in the way that I had a desire to when I first began practicing medicine in 1995. There is joy for me in knowing that what I provide to patients is a modality that treats the whole individual and honors the mind–body connection.

Figure 1.4 Patients in group helping one another to understand information. *Photo courtesy of Tamara Scott © 2005.*

> I am energized when I see patients helping each other and using their energy in supporting and assisting someone else (Figure 1.4). I feel renewed in my commitment to care when I see patients making changes in their lives that positively impact their families, their workplaces, and their communities.
>
> I highly recommend the GMA for any physician who has a desire to provide medical care for their patients in a way that treats the whole individual, for those wanting to learn and grow as people and physicians, for those who may be feeling the malaise of managed care, and for those wanting to have some fun. The group medical appointment provides all of these things and more.

Patient satisfaction and physician satisfaction have been the easiest components to measure. In all studies, patient satisfaction with GMAs has equaled or exceeded patient satisfaction with individual visits. Physicians who had only moderate or low patient satisfaction scores saw huge increases in patient satisfaction when those same patients were introduced to GMAs.

Physician satisfaction is also enhanced. The physicians that I have worked with report that GMAs are one of their favorite things to do and often the high point of their week. After doing GMAs for several years, physicians say that it would be difficult for them to practice without them. The groups become an integral part of their practices, and some even say they do not feel comfortable practicing medicine without GMAs as one of their tools.

The CHCC group is one GMA that has been studied through randomized control trials. Outcomes are discussed more thoroughly in Chapter 3.

GMAs, Chronic Disease, and Beyond

GMAs give people with chronic conditions a toolbox, education on using those tools, and action plans that produce real results in terms of both outcomes and satisfaction.

In the coming decades, these benefits will become essential. The same patients who are not being adequately served in our current system—those who need help with chronic pain, weight management, diabetes, heart disease, asthma, and other chronic diseases—are the fastest growing group of patients in health care today. As our capacity to prolong life continues to increase, they will become an even larger component of the health care picture.

GMAs are a boon for these patients, as well as for patients with other conditions that require regular, routine follow-up care: pregnancy, depression, and surgical procedures such as vasectomies, mastectomies, joint replacements. The monitoring and support components of GMAs also make them excellent vehicles for patients with a new diagnosis or new medication that must be checked frequently.

Other good GMA candidates are patients who simply want to know their physician better or who want to speak with their physician about non-emergency issues. I also suggest to physicians that they enroll their difficult or problem patients in GMAs. Patients who are particularly needy or demanding often thrive in the GMA format and use the energy they had been putting into making demands of staff into becoming positive group contributors.

What Physicians Need to Know

It is essential to stress four important facts about GMAs:

1. *The GMA is not a support group, a class, or therapy; it is a medical appointment.* Support, education, and psychological assistance occur, but physicians and staff must treat the GMA exactly the same as they treat individual appointments. Even though the GMAs provide education and support and are therapeutic, they do not take the place of classes, therapy, and support groups, but they work to enhance what is already there.
2. *The GMA is a powerful tool, but you need to plan for it and use it.* You need to prepare staff and patients for a new way of doing things and make

course corrections as necessary. You need a genuine commitment to using GMAs and a plan to make them effective.

3. *The GMA is physician-driven.* You cannot simply turn the project of instituting GMAs over to your staff. You must be the source of the energy, enthusiasm, and information in order for it to work. You need to recognize how the GMAs can best help you and your patients and then consistently use them for this purpose.
4. *GMAs are as large or small as your imagination.* I have yet to reach the boundaries of what these groups can do. Providers and organizations that use GMAs should be willing to experiment and try new ways to use these groups. In my experience, I have seen very few problems with this experimentation and generally bigger benefits to patients, providers, and organizations.

When you do the common things in life in an uncommon way, you will command the attention of the world.

George Washington Carver (1864–1943)

This is meant to say that you must want GMAs to work and make yourself the source of their success. "You need a champion to support and market these programs to patients, but the effort is well worth it," Dr Berger says.

This book gives you the tools to set up GMAs so that they transform your practice, but you cannot turn it over to your assistant, nurse, or scheduler and tell him or her to make it work. Unless both patients and staff see that it is *yours* and that it provides a treatment opportunity not served by individual appointments, I can almost guarantee that it will not succeed.

The Challenge of Change

Things do not change; we change. Henry David Thoreau, *Walden*—U.S. transcendentalist author (1817–1862)

GMAs represent an enormous change, and change is always difficult. No matter how "good" the change, we human beings seem to resist it. Sometimes we have to be dragged kicking and screaming into the house of our dreams, the relationship we have always wanted, or the professional opportunity of a lifetime.

Often the best way to keep moving forward is just to bite the bullet and focus on the benefits. When physicians are willing to let go of old ideas of what medical appointments look like and of the old paternalistic relationship with patients, they are rewarded a hundredfold. Physicians increase their own satisfaction and minimize their stress. They provide more healing to patients, without investing any more time and actually at a higher hourly rate of reimbursement, because they are seeing more patients.

Best of all, they move from a mentality of scarcity to one of abundance. They can afford to be more generous with their time and energy, to see patients more often, and to bring more of themselves to the endeavor. They can afford to be whole people with their patients and available for interaction, information, and inspiration. This is what most doctors want to do, and GMAs give them the chance to do it without sacrificing time, energy, or money.

Health care has never been static, and now it is undergoing changes. Those who are willing to challenge their old ideas, to experiment, and to succeed with new tools are those who will survive and thrive. The GMA can be a vital part of this evolution.

GMAs, however, are not "one size fits all." You need to be clear about where you are going with them and what you want them to do for you and for your practice. You need to give them a specific job and help them do it. That means monitoring how they are working for your patients, your staff, and yourself—and letting them shift with changing needs. If you do that, you can maximize both the healing you provide and your own satisfaction.

How you begin your GMA and what needs you want your GMA to address are the subjects of Chapter 2.

Chapter 2

The Many Faces of Group Medical Appointments: Which Is Right for You?

Only your imagination limits how you set up your group medical appointment (GMA).

Two broad categories of GMAs are now being used across the country:

1. *Disease- or condition-specific GMAs.* These group appointments are formed for patients with a particular disease or condition such as diabetes, chronic pain, or pregnancy.
2. *Physician-specific GMAs.* These group appointments may include a broad range of patients who have in common only the doctor they see.

Within these two broad categories, the GMA takes on many faces and forms. In this chapter, we explore some of those variations—along with the advantages and disadvantages of each kind of group. You will see a wide range of possibilities that are available with GMAs. This is meant to start your own creativity so that you can fashion a group that best suits your needs. You may come up with an entirely new GMA format.

When I first speak with people about GMAs, providers and patients try hard to get their minds around it. It is a new concept, and thus, they want to define it strictly

DOI: 10.4324/9781003673521-3

and to put it in a box so that they can understand and talk about it. I have found that it is more useful to stay a bit loose with how we define GMAs and to give them some room to grow into what works best for each individual situation and practice.

Choosing Your GMA

Think of GMAs as a problem-solving tool. When you let that tool go to wherever the problem actually exists, it becomes very powerful in your hands.

The best way to decide the most suitable kind of GMA is to define the specific challenges that you face in your practice. Then set up the group so that it addresses exactly those issues. For instance, if your practice includes many people with diabetes, you may choose a GMA for those with diabetes so that patients can share information and support, as well as the synergism and learning that occur in the group. If your challenge is access, you will want to set up a physician-specific group that allows patients to be scheduled more quickly and more frequently and for longer periods of time.

Perhaps you can see all of your patients, but their satisfaction is low. GMAs may be a way to give them the "added value" of the facilitator and the group support without taking any more of your time or energy. Maybe you are burning out with the pressure of trying to see too many patients or not being able to deal with each person in enough depth. You may need a way to make practicing medicine fun again. Let a GMA address those issues.

It is tempting to think abstractly about GMAs, rather than focusing on nut and bolt challenges in your practice. It may be tempting to run with a "good idea," something that sounds great on paper but may or may not address your specific challenges—in the end, however, GMAs that are formed to solve specific problems are usually more effective and work the best.

For instance, one physician wanted to start a GMA for women's health because she felt as though she had to repeat the same information. She thought that if she formed a group, she would only have to say it once. The group, however, never really took off. When we analyzed her practice and

BOX 2.1 GMA START-UP TASKS IN CHRONOLOGICAL ORDER

1. Understand the idea that GMA may be a helpful tool for practice.
2. Become educated on basic aspects of GMAs and begin to get a general idea of how they could be effective.
3. Present ideas to both operational and medical administration.

4. Give a presentation to the total administrative team and possibly interested physicians.
   - Look at resources currently available within the system to set this up.
   - Data—financial, access, disease outcomes.
   - Design a group that address the goals wanted to achieve in the practice.
   - Use all levels of employees to give input.
5. Assign a project manager to work with the start-up of this project.
6. Obtain consolidated business plan of resources—both staff and monetary—needed and create a timeline with tasks that include:
   - Start date of group.
   - Marketing materials.
   - Charting and scheduling mechanisms in place.
   - Space located.
   - Training for team and physicians.
   - Outcome studies planned and ready to implement.
7. Start group.
8. After every group has some time to debrief to fine-tune and discuss the experience, which is also an excellent training tool for all involved.

Source: © DeeAnn Schmucker 2006

patient load carefully, we saw that she had only about four patients a week who might qualify for the group. This was not enough to start a weekly GMA. When she actually began logging her time, she discovered that the time she had thought she was spending on women's health was actually being consumed by other issues. It had just *seemed* to her that she was repeating woman's health care information often during the week.

Questions to Ask

Here are some questions to ask when deciding what format of GMA is best for you:

- What problems do you want to solve?
- Where is your time really going?
- What is your most pressing need right now?

Solve the most pressing problem first, and then go from there. You can experiment and innovate as much as you want. You can start one kind of group, and when that is running, you can smoothly venture into other areas.

You may want to get some coaching to determine the best starting point. No "cookie-cutter" solutions are available when it comes to GMAs. Each situation is different. Thus, it can be helpful to bring some professional experience to bear on this issue so that you begin with a GMA that has been crafted to suit your specific needs.

Enlisting the support of administration in your plans for a GMA and keeping them up-to-date on progress are vital. Box 2.1 shows the steps that you will want to take in the initial planning of your group.

Start-Up Timeline for GMAs

The first item is to get administrative support for a GMA. This can take several months, as meetings tend to get full of other agenda items. Remember that this is a big shift in thinking for most. Before the presentation, send articles that speak about GMAs to the administrative team. This gives the team an opportunity to review and have a little background before the meeting. This is very important. The GMA becomes much more difficult to sell if the administrative team comes to the meeting without prior knowledge. Most of us have the tendency to say "no" initially when we are first approached about an idea in which we have no prior exposure.

The next steps are to design the type of group and to discern what needs or issues you want it to address. Getting the staff members who will directly impact the group is important in this phase. At this point, the date is set for the first GMA. In my experience, the group should begin four to six weeks after the date of that meeting. Less than four weeks makes staff feel rushed and unprepared for the group. If you wait much longer than six weeks, too much time will have passed, and more energy and work will be required to keep the concept and tasks that need to be completed in everyone's mind.

Allow extra time after the first two to four groups for the staff to meet and debrief about what happened in the group and how to be more efficient. The provider and facilitator must spend 5 minutes debriefing after each group.

When beginning a group or a pilot program, it is important that a trial time frame be established. Generally, you need three to six months to discover whether this tool will be beneficial to your practice.

The People of GMAs: Who Do You Need?

Regardless of the type of GMA instituted, many of the same roles and functions will need to be fulfilled. Often these functions can be filled with existing staff members, as part of their regular duties and additional positions probably will not be needed. These roles include the following: project manager, physician, facilitator, nurse/medical assistant, scheduler, and other allied health professionals.

Again, flexibility is important. Some groups require all of these functions, whereas others do not. Sometimes one person can fulfill several roles. The extent of these roles depends largely on how big the organization is and the number and diversity of groups. You do not need to be part of a large medical group in order to have GMAs. A single physician in a private practice can do GMAs very easily using his or her waiting room as the group room and dividing the tasks listed later in different ways. Maybe the provider performs several of these roles and the medical assistant fills other areas that need to be covered. Let the following descriptions spur your own creative thinking so that you come up with a combination of skills and functions that works for you.

Project Manager

A project manager is someone who has an administrative role in the practice. This role is vital for medical groups that have several physicians participating in GMAs. Project managers assist in overall management and allocate resources to do the group appointments. The project manager recruits staff members (either newly hired or reassigned job duties) to fulfill the roles and perform the tasks that must be completed for group appointments to occur. They must find a space to hold the group and are generally are responsible for communicating at all levels items that need to be done, for communicating outcomes, and for taking initiative in problem-solving. Again, for small or single practices, the provider who is doing the group easily assumes this role.

In large medical practices, project managers are also responsible for working with others to identify physicians that could benefit from having a GMA. Part of the identification of those providers is data gathering to see what areas of the physician's practice could most benefit from GMAs and then working with the physician and other staff members to create a group or groups to assist with the identified needs. Project managers also need to work with the physician to set up outcome studies and data collection to help guide everyone when adjustments are made to the GMA. This position alone, depending on the number of GMAs an organization has, can be a full-time position.

Physician

Physicians are the driving force behind any GMA. They usually decide to implement GMAs and decide how the group will be structured and run. Their job is to inform and persuade both staff members and patients of the value of this new tool and to make it work for staff members so that they, along with the physicians, can become ambassadors to patients. GMAs that succeed are those that have physicians who have a clear understanding of how they want their group to benefit their patients and practice and work actively for their success.

"If I were giving advice to someone who was thinking about instituting GMAs," says Dr Daniel Berger of Sansum Medical Foundation Clinic in Santa Barbara, "I would say that their champion needs to be a physician. We sometimes get so busy as practitioners that we don't want to take the time. But I'm glad I did because I love the GMA."

At the actual GMA, the physician spends about 5 to 10 minutes with each patient examining, diagnosing, reviewing medications, discussing lab or other test results, educating, and doing documentation—the same things that would happen at an individual appointment, except that 11 other patients are learning everything that the patient who is being seen is learning. In the groups that function the best, the physician keeps his or her comments minimal and uses the rest of the group to assist with health education and to discuss the benefits or possible side effects of the treatment being discussed. For example, if a patient needs to exercise to assist with the management of his or her chronic condition, the physician may say, "Does anyone here have any thoughts on how to start to exercise?" He or she may also say, "Would anyone be willing to share what he or she does for exercise?" In my experience as a facilitator for GMAs, patients are much more likely to take the advice of other patients than of the professionals in the group.

Facilitator

This role is one of the most significant "added values" that GMAs provide. It is a new component for medical appointments, and physicians love it. People who fulfill this role might be psychologists, licensed clinical social workers, marriage and family counselors, other mental health professionals, or other health professionals with good people skills. Mental health providers can be on salary or contracted. Personal coaching skills are useful, but not essential.

In addition to facilitating the GMA with physicians, the facilitator performs a variety of functions that include bringing forward any psychosocial, emotional, or behavioral issues that may be affecting patients' health; dealing with these issues or providing referrals to mental health or community resources; educating patients or inviting in "speakers" to give short, 5-minute talks on relevant subjects; and being lifestyle and behavioral coaches.

Facilitators not only add a whole new dimension to the appointment, but also can screen, refer, and provide resources that are not always at physicians' fingertips. They can help deal with difficult patients or patients with high emotional or psychological needs. They act as timekeepers and keep the group moving, but they also encourage patients to share with and support one another.

The interaction between the facilitator and physician is a dance. The facilitator listens when the patient and physician talk with one another and makes sure that any pertinent lifestyle or psychosocial issues are identified and addressed. Is there anything about the patient's living situation or other support systems that need to be adjusted? How can the group help this patient to deal with a specific problem? Again, group members are sometimes the best problem solvers because they are likely to have dealt with similar situations and can come up with practical solutions that might not occur to the facilitator or physician.

Although hiring mental health professionals as facilitators may increase the cost of providing GMAs, these costs are usually offset by the physician's capacity to see 12 people in the time that he or she might otherwise see 6 or fewer patients. If cost is prohibitive, I have seen nurses and other health professionals fulfill the facilitator role well. Some GMAs do not require facilitators depending on the makeup, structure, and desired results of the group. The Cooperative Health Care Clinic (CHCC) model does not use facilitators per se, but the team of the physician and staff works to facilitate that group. I find that having a facilitator and having that facilitator be a mental health professional are important in the primary care physician-specific GMAs where the concern that brings the patients to the appointment varies from patient to patient. Because of this, many psychosocial items are brought up and need to be addressed.

If you are in a small practice and would like to have a mental health provider as your facilitator, look in the community for someone in private practice who would be interested in contracting for a set fee per group. This is beneficial, as you can provide the service without hiring an additional employee. The benefit for the mental health professional is that he or she, like you, gets frustrated with billing insurance companies and will not have to do that. They also get a relationship with you and vice versa where referrals happen back and forth. Because of this, many are willing to do the 2 hours in the group (facilitators need to be the first person there and the last to leave, and thus, more time is required) for the price of 1 hour of private consultation.

Nurse/Medical Assistant

If a nurse or medical assistant is present, he or she takes vitals and makes sure that current lab or other test results are available for each patient. The nurse also fills an important role in assisting the facilitator in making the patients—especially new patients to the group—feel comfortable and welcome. They also are a tremendous resource for both patients and physicians in their ability to teach, to triage, to have knowledge of community resources, and to assist with the exploration of psychosocial issues. Nurses also make good facilitators; however, it is difficult to do both jobs at once.

Scheduler

This person assists patients in making appointments in a way that is similar to how other types of appointments are made. In the GMA, the scheduler may be called on to reschedule patients into the group or to offer the group to patients that the physician has identified. He or she must be well informed about GMAs and advocate for them with patients and their families.

It is vital to the success of the groups that nurses and schedulers get the opportunity to view at least one group appointment and to review the patient satisfaction surveys. Both of these disciplines assist with the promotion of the GMAs and deal with the patient's anxiety about trying something new. If nurses and schedulers do not get the opportunity to see how positively the patients' experience is of the group, they may believe these medical appointments are anxiety producing and that patients receive lower quality of care. The receptionist can also fill this role, especially if scheduling is also part of his or her daily activities.

Other Allied Health Professionals

At times, other allied health professionals (such as specialists, diabetes educators, psychologists, phlebotomists, and pharmacists) may attend the group to provide a small discussion or to answer patient questions on a particular topic. Often a small amount of time is available, and thus, these professionals need to be aware of time limits. In adult learning, people are able to go away with one to three concepts from an interaction; thus, it is important to keep that in mind when preparing for this type of presentation. Keep it simple and short.

All roles are responsible for the promotion of the GMAs. Whenever the opportunity arises, a patient must be given verbal or written information about GMAs. This is a new idea and will take some repetition and reminding for staff members as well as patients.

These common functions are performed at GMAs. Your GMA may have fewer or greater number of people. Again, set it up to meet your specific and most pressing needs.

The remainder of this chapter describes various types of GMAs in use today and the advantages and disadvantages of each. You may see one that perfectly suits your needs, or you may put together a combination of GMAs, with elements from several different GMA formats (Table 2.1).

Table 2.1 Comparison of advantages and disadvantages of GMAs

	Flexibility for both the patient and physician	*Patient Support*	*Ability to know and control the education patients receive*	*Ease of outcome collecting*	*Easier to maintain census*
Physician specific	X	X			X
PS-CHCC		X	X	X	
Disease specific		X			
DS-CHCC or same people every time		X	X	X	
DS-Different people every time	X	X			X
DS-Part of a large clinic or program	X	X	X	X	X
DS-CHCC		X	X	X	
Mixed group of new patients and follow up	X	X	X	X	
New patients	X	X			X
Physicals group		X	X		X

Source: © DeeAnn Schmucker 2006
CHCC= Cooperative Health Care Clinic
DS= Disease Specific
PS= Physician Specific

Cooperative Health Care Clinic

In these GMAs, patients are typically enrolled in the groups according to specific criteria, either disease state or age. In this type of group, the same 15 to 20 patients meet together monthly. These groups typically last 2 to 2.5 hours.

How It Works

Warmup Period: 15 Minutes

During this time, patients arrive and reconnect and socialize with each other. The nurse or physician is there to facilitate this time and to welcome the patients.

Health Education: 30 Minutes

Patients are then given a presentation on a health care topic. Some examples of topics include medications and drug-related problems, exercise, nutrition, alternatives for care, advanced directives, home safety, and the use of emergency care services. Patients select the topics ahead of time, and arrangements are made to have their physician, a guest physician, or other health professional make a presentation and hold a discussion on the chosen topic. Time is allowed for patients to ask questions and interact.

Break: 15 Minutes

This time is for patients to stretch, use the restroom, and enjoy some refreshments while they socialize. This is also an opportunity for the nurse to take vitals, blood pressure, and weights and to review the medical records to make sure that the patient is up-to-date on immunizations. Nurses also check for recent labs that the patient may need to be informed of and determine whether the patient has any needs that may need immediate attention, such as an individual appointment. At this point, if necessary, the nurse can then schedule the patient to see the physician privately and complete patient-initiated paperwork, or he or she can notify the physician if forms require physician completion. The physician makes good use of this time by mixing with patients, answering questions, and dealing with some individual concerns. This is especially valuable as patients in this informal setting are apt to tell the physician information that they might not recognize as being important (i.e., chest pain) or that they otherwise forget to mention in a time-limited individual appointment. If the patient has a question or a concern that the physician believes the other patients could also benefit from, the physician may interject into the conversation and answer that question in front of everyone.

Questions and Answers: 15 Minutes

During this time, the physician fields remaining questions and facilitates the planning for the next meeting.

Private Examinations: 60 Minutes

At this point, those patients who were identified as needing some private time with the physician are placed in examination rooms and given brief visits. Summaries of the visit are given to the patients to keep. This is added to a notebook that contains important personal medical information, such as labs and notes as well as health education information. Patients are encouraged to bring these back to each GMA so that they can be reviewed and updated by the nurse and physician.

Maintaining the census of this group may initially appear easier than other types of GMAs because of having the same patients for each group, but attendance needs to be carefully monitored in this group as well. The census for CHCC groups declines for similar reasons as in all other GMAs. Patients may change health plans, move, pass away, or decide not to continue coming, although this last reason occurs rarely. It is important to have a designated person to monitor the number of members in the group and to enroll routinely new members when the census begins to drop.

Advantages of the CHCC Model

Many unique advantages to the CHCC model of care exist.

- *Become a community for each other.* Because the patients are mostly consistent with few changes, these patients become very close to each other and provide effective support for each other that is not as readily available in our current society. With families living farther distances apart, group members can sometimes fill in some of those missing roles in support by monitoring each other and befriending each other.
- *Have consistent access to their medical information.* The notebooks or personalized medical records that the patients bring with them to each group are important. This is a great way to communicate with the patients so that both the patients and providers understand what is going on. It is excellent

for the patient to have this information in one place rather than on many separate pieces of paper that often get misplaced after they get home.

- *Results are measurable.* Because the makeup of the group varies little (compared with other group models) and there is a similar disease or situation bringing the members together, this type of GMA is excellent for randomized trials and studies. Outcomes on the CHCC model are discussed in detail in the outcome section of this book.
- *Having a chronic condition is normalized.* Patients learn that they are not alone. In society, we are often lulled into believing that we are the only ones with problems. When patients observe others with health issues, they begin to realize that this is a normal part of life. This recognition, in turn, actually often makes them feel better.
- *Fewer people and situations fall through the cracks.* Because patients come in on a regular basis, the provider and nurse can check up on them often and can be alerted to potential problems that the patient may not have noticed or brought to their attention.
- *Providers can keep better track of the information dispensed.* Because the same group meets every time and the discussion topics are decided in advance, it is easy to track and balance the information that patients are provided. I am not aware that it has been done, but it would be easy to do a knowledge survey comparing the knowledge group members have of their situation versus patients who do not attend the group.
- *Patients have a standing office visit.* For high-risk groups, this is an effective tool in diagnosing potential problems and providing treatment before the patients require more intensive care such as at an emergency department, hospital, or an extended care facility.

Disadvantages of the CHCC Model

Several disadvantages to this GMA exist. As in most cases, some of the advantages in some settings can be a disadvantage in others.

- The financial success of the CHCC model depends on major savings in big-ticket areas such as hospitalization and emergency department visits. In order to see financial gain, the provider doing the group needs to be part of an integrated health care system.
- This type of GMA is not as flexible to use as some of the other GMAs, as it occurs at the same time and only once a month; this visit is best used for maintenance or prevention. If a patient has a concern, the next GMA may be too far in the future for the patient, and that patient will need to schedule an individual appointment. This is also the case for the physician who,

wanting to provide good care, may not find it advisable for the patient to wait too long.

- This tool really does not deal very effectively with access problems. Again, meeting once a month with the same group of people does not free much schedule time for the physician, or give many patients in the practice access to care.
- Much of what constitutes access is patient perception. Other GMA types that occur at least once a week and are open to the entire practice become a viable tool for patients whether they attend the group or not. They at least perceive that if needed they can see their physician when the group is available. Their perception changes about how difficult it is to see the physician, and their sense of control over their health care increases, reducing the anxiety that occurs when getting in to see the doctor is restricted.
- This group takes some additional resources in maintaining and assessing new patients for the group.
- Because of the design of this group, the patient's concerns are often dealt with by just the physician and not in front of the others in the group. Because of this, patients may have less opportunity to benefit from the help and therapeutic value that a group can provide if the concerns are all shared openly.
- The length of the visit can be too time-consuming for the general population to use.

Physician-Specific Groups

These GMAs are not specific to any particular disease, condition, or topic, such as diabetes or depression. Usually, they are open to anyone who regularly sees a particular physician. The optimal group size is 8 to 12 patients, with the appointment typically lasting 90 minutes. Family members, caregivers, and other significant people in patients' lives are often invited. All age groups and all types of diagnoses and conditions are represented.

How It Works

Participation in all GMAs is voluntary. Thus, the physician must have a vision of what he or she wants the group to be and to communicate that vision effectively to both patients and staff.

This is how it works. Patients show up for the appointment, register, and are billed as they normally would be for an individual appointment. They come into the group room, and the co-facilitator gives an introduction and orientation that includes the following:

- What they can expect in the group, what will happen, how the doctor will proceed, some basic time frames, any ground rules that exist, and what is and is not expected of them.
- Simple logistics, such as where the bathrooms are and what is available in terms of refreshments, if any. I find that having bottled water available for the patients is an excellent choice for refreshment. Other items can be expensive and time-consuming to plan and promote eating in a society that already eats too much.
- Confidentiality. Patients are asked not to reveal the names of other patients to anyone outside the group and are asked for permission to have their own information discussed within the group. Everybody in attendance signs a confidentiality agreement (confidentiality forms and HIPAA compliance are covered in Chapter 7).
- Whether anyone needs to be seen privately by the doctor at the end of the group. New patients sometimes want this private time at first, but as they see others model the interaction in the group, by the end of the group, they usually do not feel the need for it. The "private" issues they want to discuss are often covered in the group. The physician may ask to see certain patients privately for specific issues—usually because they need an examination that requires them to disrobe or to get an EKG or some other test or procedure.
- Whether anyone needs to leave early. Sometimes new patients are somewhat uncertain and think that they might want to leave early. When the group actually gets under way, these concerns usually evaporate. Some people need to get back to work, and the physician addresses their issues first so that they can leave. Professionals really like this aspect, as they can stay as long as they wish, giving them some control of their time and how they utilize that time.

After the facilitator discusses this information, the nurse may finish taking the vital signs that were not taken before the appointment.

The physician sits next to the facilitator, and each patient is in turn asked what he or she wants to address. Other patients watch and listen as the physician conducts brief exams that can be done in a group setting, orders tests, makes referrals, prescribes new medications, answers questions, discusses lab results, fine-tunes medications, and provides general information on such topics as exercise, diet, medications, and whatever else arises in the course of the appointment.

"Personal" Issues in the Group

Patients generally are very willing to discuss personal issues in the GMA. At a recent primary care group, the first patient to speak was a woman with diabetes. She was so overweight that she had difficulty getting in and out of bed.

In a very quiet and gentle voice, she revealed that she had been suicidal for some time. The next person in the group, who had come in for hypertension, mentioned that her blood pressure was up because her son had died of alcoholism the previous week.

The stories kept coming. An Asian man with hypertension worked for a crisis line and felt that he was absorbing some of his clients' stress. He knew he needed to exercise more, but did not feel motivated. A young African American woman sitting next to him had had diabetes since she was 19 years old. She said she was afraid of leaving her children motherless and felt like a burden to her sisters, who cared for her. A neat and tidy woman with asthma in her late 60s began by saying that she liked to hike but was having soreness in her legs. The tears came when she admitted that she could not sleep at night and had a recurring memory of her father sexually assaulting her when she was a child. A woman with diabetes said that she was finally ready to address her health issues after paying off her ex-husband's $800,000 gambling debt. When painful personal experiences such as these are brought up in the group, the physician has the flexibility of time to deal with these, and more importantly, the resources of the facilitator and the group members themselves to help each other cope effectively with life experiences. Group members share their own common experiences, provide hope that the situation is survivable and conquerable, and give information on community resources for information and support. When this happens, the physician or facilitator in the group can direct the conversation from the other patients in the group to help the patient with problem-solving.

Here is another example. During a discussion about arthritis, a little voice in the back of the room said, "You mean I'm going to have to live with this! How am I going to live with this?" The lady right beside her held up her badly deformed rheumatoid hands and said, "Honey, at the break I'll tell you how to live with it."

In a typical, rushed 10- or 15-minute appointment, it is unlikely that any of this information would have surfaced. Patients would have felt compelled to keep their questions brief and limit what they said to medical issues. In the supportive atmosphere of the GMA, however, and with the luxury of 90 minutes, they are no longer just "diabetics" and "asthmatics." They are whole people, the sum total of all of their physical and emotional experiences. Patients are complete human beings who can now be treated as such.

Group Support

Trust one who has gone through it.

Virgil, *The Aeneid*, Roman epic poet (70–19 BC)

I hear and I forget. I see and I remember. I do and I understand. Real knowledge is to know the extent of one's ignorance.

Confucius

Patients thrive in this supportive GMA environment. They are generous in supporting others in the group—not only with empathy, but also with knowledge and resources. In the previously mentioned group, the crisis-line worker gently suggested Al-Anon meetings to the woman whose son had died of alcoholism so that she could separate her grief from the guilt that she was feeling. The co-facilitator asked members of the group whether they had any ideas to motivate the crisis-line worker to exercise. Several patients shared how they had inspired themselves to become more active.

The woman whose ex-husband was addicted to gambling reminded the doctor to write "insulin dependent" on the African American woman's prescription for a glucometer so that it would be covered by Medicare. Drawing on her work experience in the state disability department, she told the suicidal woman which forms she would need in order to be placed on permanent disability. The African American woman was gently led by the facilitator to focus on the here and now and to list the resources that she had available to maximize the quality of her life. For example, one resource that she had not thought of was a convenient bus line near her home that took her to community diabetic support groups.

The physician commented, "See. This is why I love group appointments. I learn something from you every time."

Although discussions are often intimate and significant, patients also like having a place to bring up everyday concerns, such as restless sleep or sore knees. Patients, physicians, and staff usually leave a GMA feeling satisfied and supported. They have a sense of contribution and of being able to give and receive help. They have spent 90 uninterrupted minutes completely devoted to healing. Whatever their part in the GMA happens to be, they almost always feel that the appointment was a rich experience. For physicians, this kind of GMA can provide an entirely new perspective on how they practice medicine.

Advantages of the Physician-Specific Model

This group is powerful for several reasons:

- *The beneficial principles and behaviors suggested for one patient usually apply to everyone in the group, regardless of their disease or condition.* For example, the diet for a person with diabetes is good for anyone. The exercise program for a heart patient is good for everyone. Stress management works the same way regardless of the source of the stress or its effect. Patients' conditions and medications may be different, but the level of cross-education is extremely high in this kind of group.
- *Patients learn that they are not alone and that others may be even worse off than they are.* When patients go into a GMA with a wide variety of diagnoses, most of them walk away feeling lucky. No matter how sick they are, they do not have what the other person has. An older gentleman expressed this very concept when he confided in a focused group session on the benefits of group visits. "I look around me, and I see all these folks with all these problems and it makes me feel pretty good … even though I feel terrible."
- Patients get the experience of seeing their physician treat illnesses other than their own, and thus, they feel more confident in their provider's skills—and also feel as if they know the doctor better.
- *The GMA is an excellent forum for complete, holistic care and education.* People are treated not simply as disease states, but as whole human beings, and they develop the skills, education, and attitudes to approach their own self-care from this point of view. They also learn about diseases or conditions that are not their primary diagnosis, but may be related to it. For instance, patients with diabetes often have arthritis, heart problems, or depression as well. They learn that these conditions often overlap and how to prevent them or deal with them when they do occur, or they may have family members with the same conditions as other members of the group and are grateful for the increased understanding that they get in the group.
- *Patients can share practical solutions either because they have been in the same situation or because some solutions are effective regardless of the disease.* I have seen a patient with asthma help a patient with diabetes, for instance, because both were young mothers and had to cope with caring for children in the midst of their disease.
- This is the most flexible of all group types for both patients and physicians.
- *Patients' perception of having access to their physician increases.* With the onset of managed care, patients have experienced a loss of control over when they see their physician and how much time the physician has to spend with them. We know this loss of control makes patients anxious, and that often increases the symptoms to unbearable heights. With our current system, patients sometimes feel that they need to make appointments ahead of time "just in case" they will need to be seen, as they do

not feel that they can rely on our current system to have appointment time available when a need arises. With this type of group, patients know that they can get in to see the physician at a minimum of seven days (fewer days if the provider has more groups per week). This reduces their anxiety and concern. They perceive that they have some control and that the physician will be able to see them within a reasonable amount of time. Knowing when that time is and planning for it also gives them the perception of control, thus the perception of access.

- *This model as well as many of the other models of GMAs actually creates space for providers.* For example, perhaps the provider is not able to keep up with the demand for initial consults. By putting follow-up patients in GMAs, time is actually created to assist the physicians in working down their backlog of initial consults.

Disadvantages of the Physician-Specific Model

The greatest challenge with this group is that it requires the most significant shift in perception—of what medical care looks like and of what the relationship between physician and patient should be. To make this GMA effective, providers must think outside the box. After this group is in place, however, it usually works very well for everyone. Patients, physicians, and staff wonder how they managed without it. This group also tends to be the most challenging in which to measure results using randomized trials.

Disease- or Condition-Specific Groups

In these groups, all of the patients have the same diagnosis or condition. These conditions might include diabetes, depression, cancer, hypertension, pregnancy, or surgical procedures.

These groups share many of the features of physician-specific GMAs, except that there may be a 5-minute presentation at the beginning of the appointment on a specific topic highlighting two or three key points related to the patients' common illness or condition. This short talk is given either by the physician or by another medical professional.

These GMAs can work in a variety of ways.

Same People Every Time

In this type of group, the same 12 people have an appointment at specific, regular intervals.

These GMAs are wonderful opportunities for education. I worked with a northern California Air Force base to develop a group appointment for patients with diabetes. We invited someone from the lab to explain HbA1c to the group. While the group was in session, the patients had their blood drawn for their HbA1c in a chair that was in the same room, but just outside of the group circle. Patients could get their labs done without waiting and did not miss any education or support that was happening in the group. When patients understood more about what their lab work meant and why it was important, they became more proactive about it. They did not have to be followed as often. This took the pressure off the physician, staff, and others who had been riding hard on them to get their labs done.

The next month, the topic might focus on diet. A dietitian, using a handout for the patient's future reference, would give 5 minutes of tips on healthy eating and possibly offer some health foods to sample. Another month, the podiatrist might come to examine all of the patients' feet, trim nails, and discuss good care for their feet, problems to look for, and when to see the podiatrist.

After the 5- to 10-minute talk, the physician speaks with each patient in the group setting and addresses labs, questions, concerns, needs, and medications. Education is intense because everybody in the group has the same condition. Whatever the physician says to one patient usually applies to everyone.

Advantages of Having the Same People Every Time

This type of GMA gives patients not only education, but also the following:

- There is an excellent support system. They get to know one another well and contribute to one another with both information and emotional support.
- They often remember the action items each person committed to taking and hold each other accountable for the completion of those items and help the patient solve problem when his or her action items were not completed. The physician knows what information these patients have and do not have—thus, he or she can reinforce it in subsequent groups or in individual appointments.

Disadvantages of Having the Same People Every Time

- There is not much flexibility in scheduling with this type of group. The time is set and cannot be changed to suit either the physician's or the patients' individual needs. The patients therefore cannot use the group as a replacement for an individual appointment if they need to be seen sooner than the next scheduled meeting of the group; thus, it does not cut down on the number of individual appointments as in some of the other models.

- Sometimes these groups are set up as time limited so that patients at the onset, for example, agree to come to the group once a month for six consecutive months. The problem with this is that often the group members do not want to give up the group after they are finished with the six sessions and then feel abandoned.
- Another potential challenge is that when patients first come to the group from another physician and the GMA doctor makes a suggestion or changes their medication, the patient may want to go back to the original physician to discuss the changes. Some patients do not feel right until they have talked with their "real doctor." The original physician needs to be very clear that "Dr Smith (who is running the GMA) will be treating your diabetes until you have improved, and then you may return to my care." If this is clear at the beginning, fewer problems occur.

Different People Every Time

This group appointment meets at the same time every week, and patients access it as needed. It always addresses the specific disease for which it was formed, but the patients who attend may vary from week to week.

Patients come to this group on a "need to see" basis. For example, a physician may put a patient on a new medication and ask that he or she come back to the group the following week to follow-up on how the medication is working, or the patient may commit to an action plan that brings about a change in lifestyle. These patients need to be seen in two to three weeks to hold them accountable for their action plan. Other patients may not need to be seen for several months. If patients want to be seen sooner than the physician requested, they can schedule to attend the group at an earlier date.

Advantages: Same Disease, Different People

This group's flexibility makes it an effective tool for both patients and the physicians. Patients feel more relaxed about their treatment because the group is available whenever they need it. They know that they will never have to wait more than a week to get their questions or concerns addressed. They also enjoy the support, the exposure to other patients, and the educational opportunities.

Disadvantages: Same Disease, Different People

With patients coming and going, knowing what education or disease management information patients have already received can be difficult. Although we really never know what information patients retain, we do know what information we presented.

GMAs as Part of a Larger Clinic or Program

In this setting, the GMA is one of many tools used to manage a specific disease. One medical group began using GMAs as part of a larger chronic pain program. Patients were examined in individual appointments for the initial consult and then were placed in a GMA as part of the program. The physician who ran the GMA became the doctor to treat their pain. The expectation was that unless there was a special need to see the physician individually, all patients would receive care from the physician in the group. Patients in this program also had an opportunity to participate in the following:

- An 8-week educational course on chronic pain that emphasizes coping tools.
- Training on a neurobehavioral tool that taught them how to shut the pain gates.
- Physical therapy.
- Psychotherapy.

The GMA provided reinforcement of the rest of the program, along with physician care.

Another medical group in northern California used its database to identify people with diabetes who had high HbA1c or who were not up-to-date on their HbA1c. They called these people to schedule them for blood work and at the same time asked whether they had had any diabetic education and asked them to sign up for a GMA.

During this group, the physician and the facilitator, who was a diabetes educator, reviewed the lab results and provided a great deal of education on how different drugs work with blood sugar. They stressed the importance of making lifestyle changes and coached the patients in setting small, specific goals for these changes.

The group also acted as a screening tool for referrals to other resources and classes. Some patients had already used these resources and became powerful advocates for them with other patients.

Advantages of Having a GMA as Part of a Larger Program

GMAs are good opportunities for education and often become screening tools to assess patients' needs for other community-based services or referrals such as classes, support groups, physical therapy, and psychotherapy.

Disadvantages of Having a GMA as Part of a Larger Program

To make the organizational effort for this type of GMA worthwhile, a large panel of patients with the specific disease is needed.

Mixed Group of New Patients and Follow-Ups

This kind of group mixes new patients with "old" patients who have already started treatment for a specific condition. One podiatrist uses this kind of GMA for chronic heel pain. Before the group, he examines new patients in individual exam rooms and explains that he will answer questions in the group. Six follow-up patients are waiting in the GMA room when they arrive.

The physician begins by discussing the general causes and treatments of heel pain. Follow-up patients are already involved in some of these treatments and can share their successes with the new patients. They talk about what they have done and what has worked; thus, the new patients begin their treatment with more confidence. The group usually takes 45 to 60 minutes from the time of the initial consults to finish.

Obstetricians and midwives have used this kind of GMA for prenatal checks. They mix women who are coming in for their first visits, about their first pregnancies, with women who are at different stages of their pregnancies and/or who have had multiple pregnancies. During the first part of the group, the physician usually listens to the babies' heartbeats behind a screen while a facilitator presents a short talk and discussion. The physician and facilitator then address each woman's issues. The women learn from listening to the physician interact with other group members and are also an excellent source of information and support for one another.

A urologist uses these GMAs to discuss vasectomy surgery. Patients get general information and ask questions in the group so that everybody benefits from the learning. Exams are conducted privately.

Advantages of Mixed Group with New Patients and Follow-Ups

New patients learn from patients who have had more experience. They are often more willing to comply with treatments because the follow-up patients have shared their success. The questions that patients bring to the group prompt discussions that become an important source of information for everyone.

Disadvantages of Mixed Group with New Patients and Follow-Ups

This type of GMA may not have much flexibility, either for patients or for physicians, and thus, the staff must be very conscientious about scheduling patients in the group to ensure that the group is well used.

New Patients

GMAs initially were not recommended for new patients, for confused patients, or for patients speaking a different language than the one spoken during the group. However, I have witnessed all of these patients attending GMAs with some level of success. We found that although the confused patients did not get anything more from a GMA than an individual appointment, often their caregiver did. Also, those with a hearing impairment can benefit from the group if they have someone along to sign for them and assist with the communication. New patients can be treated very effectively in GMAs, especially if all of the patients are new. It is distracting, however, to have a translator in the GMA if the language used in the group is not known to the patient.

The Veterans Administration Hospital in Reno, Nevada, made good use of the new patient model to solve some of their immediate problems and to serve their patients needs. One of the underserved areas this group experienced was in providing timely access to veterans who wanted to use the Veterans Administration for their medical care and/or prescription benefits. The individual initial consult for new patients generally took an hour of the providers' time. The physicians' schedule was already overbooked in seeing the patients already enrolled in the system.

A GMA was established for the new patients so that they could be enrolled in the system and start receiving their drug benefits. The flow of the new patient group went like this: New patients checked in and were taken to the group room by a nurse who gave them forms to complete and took their vital signs. When this was complete, the physician came into the room and collected data from patients by asking them questions as a group and recording their answers. For example, the physician may have asked, "Does anyone here drink?" Then everyone took turns discussing the amount of alcohol or other substances they use. When the general questions were asked, the physician then asked each patient in turn about his or her medical conditions. While the physician was doing that, a pharmacist checked the patients currently prescribed medication to see whether it was on the Veterans Administration formulary and suggested possible substitutions if not listed. The physician then took each patient into a room for a brief physical examination while the group discussed common issues.

Instead of seeing one new patient per hour, physicians were able to see four to five new patients in 90 minutes, saving themselves time and providing a quality interaction for the patient. Another benefit for these patients was that after the group was completed they were able to go to the pharmacy and pick up their medication without a lengthy wait.

Advantages of the New Patient GMA

- *It greatly assists in reducing access problems.* Patients can get scheduled into their initial appointment very quickly.
- *Patients are very open about sharing personal information.* Patients opened up easily about the substance abuse and other personal problems as others encouraged them. I am often asked by professionals if patients keeping confidentiality is a problem. In Chapter 7, HIPAA and confidentiality are discussed in greater detail. Several things need to be taken into consideration when looking at this: First, mental health has been doing therapy groups for years, having patients sign an agreements and deal with the most sensitive of issues in these groups with documented success; second, we have patients sit in waiting rooms—talking to each other, filling out forms, speaking with staff, recognizing each other—and we as medical professionals do not typically worry about confidentiality; measures are taken to preserve confidentiality (described in detail in Chapter 7).
- *It gives patients a good introduction to GMAs.* Patients now know how groups work and soon learn how to use this as a tool for themselves in managing their health care.

Disadvantages of the New Patient GMA

- The patients who attend this GMA often want to continue to have this option available for their other visits and are frustrated when and if this is not an option.
- After attending this type of GMA, the patient often wants to use the physician who participated in the GMA as his or her primary care physician.

Physicals

This model is composed of a private physical examination, and then explanation and discussion occur in the group. This model of GMA can be used for annual physicals, joint replacements, or other conditions that require an examination where disrobing may be a factor.

Here is an example of what a physicals group could look like:

- Patient checks in and pays the co-pay, if applicable.
- Patient is then taken to an exam room, where the nurse takes the patient's vital signs and asks the patient to disrobe.
- The physician comes in and spends about 5 minutes doing the procedure/examination and lets the patient know that he or she can expect to have his or her questions answered in the group room with the other patients.
- The patient then gets dressed and goes to the group room where the physician then addresses each patient's concerns.

Generally, the patients ask similar questions, thus giving the physician the opportunity to answer questions once without repeating himself or herself numerous times throughout the day.

Advantages of Physicals GMA

This model has some of the same advantages as the new patient model.

- *It greatly assists in reducing access problems.* Patients can get scheduled into their initial appointment very quickly.
- *Patients are very open about sharing personal information.* Patients open up easily about the substance abuse and other personal problems, as they are encouraged by others.
- It gives patients a good introduction to GMAs.
- It lets the physician give important information to the patients once instead of repeating it throughout the day.

Disadvantages of Physicals GMA

- *This group meets only once.* Very often after experiencing this group, patients would like to have the opportunity to attend other groups for part of their medical care.

- *This requires more involvement from the staff.* The staff needs to keep track of where the patients are in the process and provide direction for them in where to go next.

In order to get a visual picture and do a comparison of the advantages and disadvantages of these differing GMA types, please see Table 2.1.

Snapshots

The following are some snapshots of various kinds of GMAs. They may serve as a springboard for thinking about your own GMA.

Diabetes Management

An innovative GMA was developed to manage type 2 diabetes for patients at a medical group in California. The program reaches out to patients who are

- Newly diagnosed.
- Having difficulty complying with the standard patient care interventions.
- Starting insulin.
- Dealing with other health conditions as well as diabetes.

A patient care coordinator contacts these patients, and a physician and a social worker lead this group. Patients get intensive medical management, education, and discussion about lifestyle and psychosocial factors, as well as support from both care providers and fellow patients. Pharmacists, nutritionists, diabetic educators, podiatrists, and physical therapists are also involved in the group.

Pain Management Program

A medical group in Davis, California, offers a GMA as part of a comprehensive neurological pain management program. Its purpose is to empower patients toward functional independence and to enhance the quality of their lives. Each patient sees a neurologist, attends a chronic pain class taught by a registered nurse and licensed clinical social worker, has sessions with a physical therapist, and can also learn alternative techniques for pain management. The GMA allows patients to learn more about their condition, be evaluated on follow-up, benefit from one another's personal experience, and have access to a ready-made support system.

Depression Management Group

Another medical group developed a depression management group in response to feedback from physicians about the need for access to mental health services in the community. The purpose of this group is for patients to gain control over their condition. They are given general education about depression, management skills, and a supportive forum where they can practice these skills. This group is an adjunct to therapy and medication management.

The group is also designed to help doctors deal with the unique needs of these patients in their panels. The primary care physicians were happy to have a place to refer their patients with depression and were especially excited about behaviorists being available to help manage these patients.

We are finding that depression management lends itself particularly well to GMAs. Some reasons for this are as follows:

- Depression still carries a certain stigma, and thus, people are not well educated about it.
- People who are depressed tend to be isolated, and thus, the group is of particular benefit.
- Their medications need to be monitored and adjusted regularly.

Each appointment includes a 5-minute educational talk, group discussion and sharing about the topic, and the formulation of an action plan around some aspect of the topic. Patients implement the plan over the next week and report back to the group. The co-facilitator sends a progress note to the referring primary care physician, along with the patient's action plan. The physician can then follow-up with the patient and reemphasize the benefits of keeping with the program.

Patients who attended the group reaffirm the belief in its value. The survey conducted by Sutter Medical Foundation in 2003 of patients participating in this group found that

- Patients need to feel in control of their lives and their condition. The primary reasons that they gave for attending the group were to learn, to interact with others, and to feel more in control of their lives.
- Physicians have a greater influence on whether patients join the group, on whether they stay in the group, and on how well they cope than originally anticipated.
- Support from fellow patients and the group bonding experience plays an important role in the healing process.

- Having hobbies and community participation and, to a lesser extent, relying on support from family and friends were also listed as methods of coping with depression.
- Patients had a mixed response to the didactic approach and action plans. Some patients felt that they benefited considerably from this structured approach, whereas others felt that the approach did not leave enough room for free-flowing discussion.
- Early dropouts were patients who had come to the group with preconceived ideas about depression management techniques. Dealing with their concerns at the outset would have contributed to their acceptance of the program and their success with it.
- It was also revealed that the program would work better if it were less structured and also if it were offered in the evenings and on weekends.

This kind of follow-up study is essential. GMAs must be responsive to patients' medical, psychological, and logistical needs. That means they must stay open to change and adjustment. (This particular group did not include a billing provider in it, but this same structure can be done with a billing provider.)

Prenatal Group

A nurse midwife runs a prenatal GMA for expectant mothers and their partners. In this open atmosphere, people want to talk about *everything* related to childbearing. First-time mothers share the group with experienced mothers, who can partner with the nurse midwife in educating the new mothers.

"I enjoyed being in the presence of other pregnant women and also to be able to talk with the midwife in a time-relaxed environment," said one patient. Questions and concerns relate not just to pregnancy and labor, but also to the postpartum period.

Point Your GMA toward Your Problems

Choose the type of group you do carefully, and point it toward solving your most pressing problems. Typically, medical groups and physicians start with a pilot. They learn as they go and make whatever changes are necessary so that the group works for everyone. As the GMA develops a history and a following, more and more patients want to attend, and other physicians get interested in starting groups.

Chapter 3

Outcome Studies

Outcomes on group medical appointments (GMAs) have been and are being done, and more will be done. Because this tool has not been recognized as part of medical care, it has not yet been widely studied. Seeing a group firsthand gives the observer a great amount of anecdotal information, as the excitement, care, support, and willingness of the patients to try new behavior show National Committee of Quality Assurance (NCQA), many of the benefits of the GMAs. Some of the outcomes are used throughout this book to show success and also to show examples of how to use this tool. This chapter gives a brief glimpse at some of the studies that have been completed.

Cooperative Health Care Clinic

At this time, more studies, especially randomized trials, have been done on the Cooperative Health Care Clinic (CHCC) model than on the many other GMA models.

This occurs for several reasons:

- The CHCC model has been used since 1991.
- The structure of this GMA lends itself to a randomized study, as the population and the numbers of times in group and the education provided in the group setting are more trackable.

DOI: 10.4324/9781003673521-4

Other GMAs have not been around as long; in fact, new ways of doing GMAs are being planned every day. Studies have been started on these newer groups, but we first discuss some of the studies on the CHCC model.

The first published article (Beck et al., 1997) of a randomized, controlled study on group medical appointments reported the results of the CHCC model of care, which was designed by a team that Dr Scott at Kaiser in Denver, Colorado, headed. The objective of this study was to compare the impact of group outpatient visits to the traditional individual visits on health service utilization and cost, self-reported health status, and patient and physician satisfaction. Participants included 321 health maintenance organization members aged 65 years and older who had chronic illness and had relatively high health care utilization within the prior 12 months. High utilization was defined as one or more outpatient visits per month and one or more calls to the nurse or physician every two months. Eligible patients were sent a letter inviting their participation in a research study. Interested patients were randomized to either the intervention group with group appointments or "usual care," where participants saw their physician in traditional individual appointments. A total of 160 participants were randomized to group visits and 161 to usual care. To account for differences in physician practice style, randomization was done within the physician's practice (Figure 3.1).

The intervention went as follows: Patients assigned to the intervention had monthly group visits with their physician and nurse. These monthly group visits included a 15-minute socialization period followed by a 30-minute health education presentation on a specific health-related topic. Time was allowed for patient questions and answers. During the next 15 minutes, the nurse took blood pressure readings and reviewed patients' medical records for needed immunizations and immediate medical care needs. The physician circulated and attended to individual concerns that the patients raised.

A period of questions and answers and planning for the next meeting was followed by 30 minutes for the physician to conduct one-on-one visits with patients.

Patients were tracked for one year. Outcome measurements showed that participants in the group had fewer emergency department visits (p = .009), fewer visits to subspecialties (p = .028), and fewer repeat hospitalizations per patient (p = .051). Group participants made more visits (p = .021) and calls to nurses (p = .038) than the control group patients and fewer calls to the physician (p = .019). In addition, a greater percentage of group participants received influenza and pneumonia vaccinations ($p < .001$). Group patients had greater overall satisfaction with care (p = .019) (Table 3.1). No difference was noted between groups on patients' self-reported health or functional status. The cost of care per member per month was $14.79 less for the group participants, with most of the

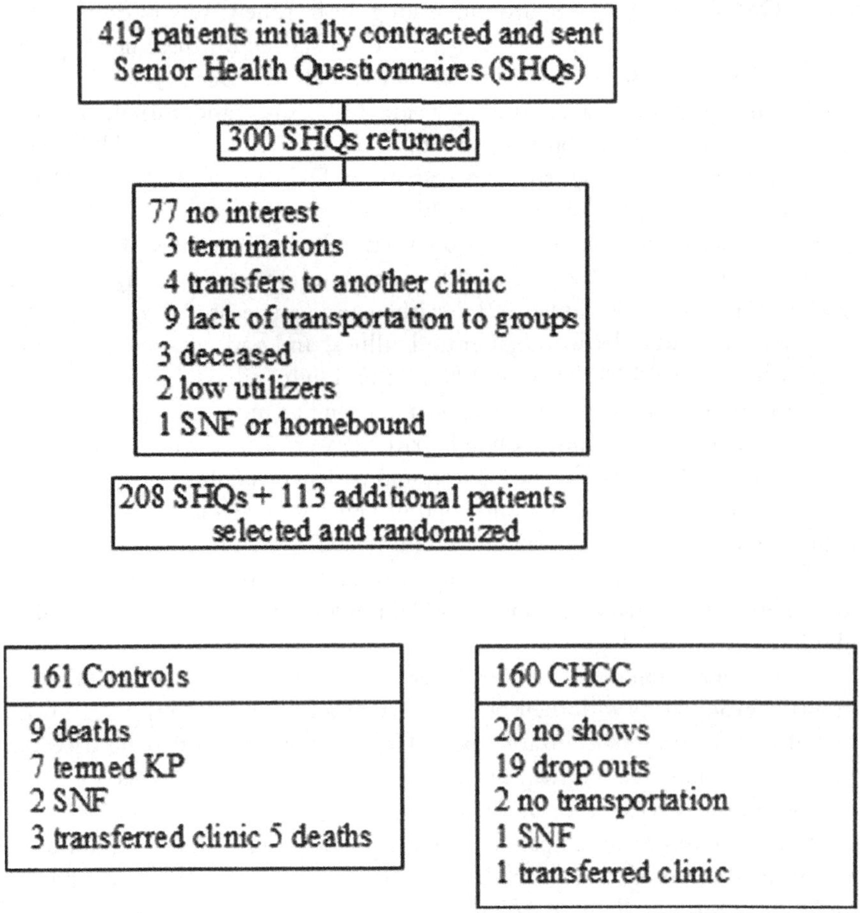

Figure 3.1 A randomized trial of group outpatient visits for chronically ill older HMO members: The cooperative health care clinic. *Source*: ***JAGS*** **45: 543–549; 1997, the American Geriatrics Society.**

cost savings being attributed to fewer emergency department visits and skilled nursing facility use.

Physician satisfaction was measured between the five internal medicine physicians who participated in the CHCC model and the 42 internal medicine physicians that did not. CHCC physicians reported that they both greatly enjoyed treating older patients and were extremely satisfied with their ability to treat patients. Fewer than 30% of the regular internal medicine physicians reported that they greatly enjoyed treating older patients, and fewer than 5%

Table 3.1 Study outcomes

Visits	*Control mean*	*n = 161 Std Dev*	*CHCC mean*	*n = 160 Std Dev*	*P*
CHCC	N/A		6.62	4.2	
Specialist MD visits	3.95	4.93	3.22	3.51	.028
Nurse visits	1.89	2.55	2.63	2.82	.021
Emergency departments	0.67	1.62	0.41	0.87	.009
Calls in to nurse	7.89	8.21	8.7	8.95	.038
Calls returned by physicians	2.53	4.86	1.4	2.16	.019
Readmissions per patient, if hospitalized	1.89	1.3	1.43	0.78	.051

Source: JAGS 45: 543–549; 1997, the American Geriatrics Society.

of these physicians reported being extremely satisfied with their ability to treat older patients.

A follow-up randomized study of the CHCC model was conducted between 1995 and 1998. A study (Scott et al., 2004), conducted at Kaiser Permanente in the Colorado region, included 294 patients who expressed a strong interest in group visits. They were a subset of the 793 patients who were enrolled in the 2-year study.

The objective of this study was to compare the effectiveness of CHCC group visits for chronically ill health maintenance patients to usual care to evaluate differences in health care utilization, including clinic visits, inpatient admissions, emergency department use, patient satisfaction, quality of life, self-efficacy, and activities of daily living. Study patients received primary care from 19 physicians who practiced at nine different outpatient clinics. Eligible patients were randomized to the CHCC model or usual care, and randomization was done within each physician's group of patients.

Patients randomized to CHCC attended a monthly group medical appointment that included a 15-minute socialization period, a 30-minute discussion of a health-related topic, a 20-minute care-giving period, during which time the nurse took blood pressure measures and reviewed charts for immunization, laboratory tests, and immediate health care needs. The physician responded to minor patient concerns, refilled prescriptions, and responded to individual needs. Fifteen minutes was dedicated to a question-and-answer session, with an additional 10 minutes to plan for the next meeting. After the group session, a 60-minute period was available for patients to meet with the physician for individual appointments.

Patients were followed for 24 months. Compared with the patients receiving usual care, group visit patients had fewer emergency department visits ($p = .008$) and fewer inpatient admissions ($p = .013$) and used fewer professional services ($p = .005$). There was no difference in the numbers of clinic visits, pharmacy refills, outpatient hospital visits, observation units, skilled nursing facilities, or home health visits. Overall cost savings for CHCC patients over the 24-month study was $41.80 per member per month. Scores for patient satisfaction with their physician were higher for CHCC patients ($p = .22$), and these patients reported greater satisfaction with talking to their physicians about advance directives ($p < .001$); self-efficacy ratings for communicating with their physician was significantly greater ($p = .03$). CHCC patients also reported an overall higher quality of life ($p = .002$).

Coleman et al. (2001) conducted a randomized trial of emergency room utilization by chronically ill older adults who participated in group visits. The objective of this 2-year randomized trial conducted at Kaiser Permanente, Colorado, was to determine whether primary care group visits reduce emergency department utilization in chronically ill older adults; 295 adults 60 years of age or older with frequent utilization of outpatient services and one or more chronic conditions were enrolled. Those randomized to the intervention group attended monthly group visits with a primary care physician. Visits emphasized self-management of chronic illness, peer support, and regular contact with their primary care team. On average, patients in the intervention group had fewer emergency department visits ($p = .0005$) and were less likely to have any emergency department visits ($p = .003$) than controls.

Randomized trials have also been conducted for patients with specific diseases who attended group visits. A study by Sadur et al. (1999) describes the results of holding diabetes group visits for patients with type 2 diabetes with recent A1C of more than 8.5% who had not had A1C within the past year. Monthly 2-hour group visits were held over a period of six months. Sessions were offered by a diabetes nurse educator with support from a dietician health behaviorist and pharmacist. Consultative support was available from two diabetologists. Attending patients showed improved diet control, improved self-efficacy, and satisfaction with care. Patients also had decreased utilization of health care services.

Trento et al. (2001) described the results of a 2-year randomized controlled trial of 112 patients with type 2 diabetes conducted in Turin, Italy. This study showed that patients who underwent group consultation compared with those who underwent individual visits plus support education had lower A1C ($p < .002$), improved knowledge of diabetes ($p < .001$), improved quality of life ($p < .001$), and more appropriate health behaviors ($p < .001$). Physicians spent less time seeing nine to ten patients as a group than individually, but patients had longer interaction with health care providers.

In 2003, Clancy, Cope, Magruder, Huang, Saiter, and Fields at the University of South Carolina tested the feasibility and acceptability of group visits for delivering care to uninsured and inadequately insured diabetic patients with a grant from the Robert Wood Johnson Foundation. One hundred twenty patients with uncontrolled type 2 diabetes were randomly assigned to receive care in group visits or usual care for six months. Patients receiving care in groups reported improved trust in their physicians. A tendency existed for patients in group visits to report better coordination of their care, better community orientation, and more culturally competent care.

Other Types of Groups

Many studies are being done on the newer types of GMAs as well, although to my knowledge no completely randomized trials have been completed. Although trends are obvious and documented, strict randomized scientific research is difficult for several reasons:

1. *Shifting populations make it difficult.* Depending on the GMA model, patients may come to the group only once or twice a year, whereas others may come much more frequently depending on their need. The groups are being used by physicians and patients depending on the issues the patient needs addressed and the forum in which they can best be addressed. For example, if disrobing is required, then an individual appointment is generally the best treatment modality for the treatment of this issue.
2. *Because GMAs are voluntary, it is impossible to do a randomized trial.* With GMAs being so new, in most populations, it is desirable for patients to have the option of attending the group. Although we can recommend the group, just as we recommend laboratory workups and other diagnostic tests, patients still have the opportunity to refuse the medical advice recommended.
3. *Change is difficult, and GMAs are only now emerging as an answer.* Many organizations are just beginning their pilot programs. With time, as

medical groups make this a regular part of their operations, it will be easier to gather hard data.
4. *It is often costly and time-consuming to do a complete and thorough study.* With all of the new initiatives that organizations are taking to make a better, cost-effective product, time, energy, and financial resources are stretched.

Because of these, I call the outcomes of most studies "trends." We can document trends toward better patient knowledge of their conditions; decreases in pain medications, especially narcotics; lowering of blood pressure, especially in pain patients; weight loss; and increased exercise.

One unpublished study of a GMA for diabetics at the Sansum Medical Foundation Clinic in Santa Barbara compared the baseline HbA1c of 40 patients before starting the GMA with their HbA1c levels six months after attending the GMA. The HbA1c levels went from an average of 7.46 to an average of 7.06 in just six months. Results also indicated blood pressure decreased, pain decreased, use of narcotics decreased, and compliance with treatment increased.

Knowledge Studies

Patient information regarding their knowledge of their disease and treatment of this disease has also been studied with GMAs in an unpublished study at Sutter Medical Foundation in 2001. Sutter Medical Foundation and its partnering physician groups treat a vast variety of patients in a large geographical area. The patients in this study resided in one of the following types of communities: inner-city/downtown area, small mountain communities, rural farming communities, the suburbs, and a university setting. The objective of this study was to compare a physician's GMA participants with the same physician's patients who have only attended individual appointments to see whether patients who attended GMAs know more about how to care for themselves than patients who had never attended a GMA. The study focused on patients with hyperlipidemia and diabetic patients. Participating in this study were five family practice physicians who had open, physician-specific GMAs. Data were gathered from each physician comparing their patients that had attended at least one GMA with those patients in their practice who had never attended a GMA.

A 10-question test was developed for each disease state and mailed to the patient participants. In order to have a good sample size, all patients who had attended one or more GMAs in the calendar year and had high cholesterol and/or diabetes were sent a test in the mail with a self-addressed, stamped envelope. Patients who had not attended a GMA were randomized, and those chosen were mailed a test. Patients were instructed to return the test when it was completed. Patients who had only been seen in individual appointments were randomly selected from each physician's panel to participate in the study and were also sent the tests. For both diseases, GMA patients were statistically more likely to engage in regular exercise and eat a healthy diet than their counterparts who had not attended groups.

Satisfaction Studies

Patient and physician satisfaction studies are relatively easy to do, and satisfaction is often studied in conjunction with GMAs. In almost all surveys, patient satisfaction for their experience in GMAs was equal to or higher than in individual appointments.

Patient Satisfaction

In a study of the GMA pilot program at Sutter Medical Foundation, patients were asked to rate their satisfaction with the GMA by responding to seven questions on a 5-point Likert scale using excellent (5), very good (4), good (3), fair (2), and poor (1). The questions asked about the following: the length of time from making the appointment to actually seeing the physician; the length of time the patient had to wait in the office before seeing the physician; the quality of the visit; explanation of medical procedures, tests, and drugs; the amount of time with the doctor and staff; the personal interest the doctor and staff had for the patient; and the overall quality of care.

The satisfaction surveys came back very high with the overall average score of 4.67 out of a possible 5 (Table 3.2).

In another study, this time studying a new patient appointment model, a satisfaction questionnaire was given to the patients before the group started and then after the completion of the GMA. Patients were surveyed on availability of the appointment, amount of time with the physician, courtesy and helpfulness, explanation of what was done, personal manner, and visit overall, again using a 5-point Likert scale using excellent (5), very good (4), good (3), fair (2), and poor (1). In addition, this survey had patients rate their perception of health on this same scale and rate whether they would recommend this visit type to others.

As shown in Table 3.3, patients rated their actual experience much higher than their anticipated experience of the group. They also recommended the group at a higher rate after actually having the group experience (Table 3.4). What is most interesting, however, about this survey is the question on perception of

Table 3.2 Patient satisfaction data for four Pilot GMAs

Physician	*Number of surveys*	*Average score range for all questions (out of 5)*
Dr A	75	4.3–4.7
Dr B	42	4.7–4.9
Dr C	33	4.5–4.8
Dr D	62	4.4–4.8
Overall Average Score		4.67/5

Source: Noffsinger, E., and Atkins, T. (2001, April). Assessing a group medical appointment program: A case study at Sutter Medical Foundation. *Group Practice Journal.*

health. As you can see, their perception of their health changed drastically from the beginning of the group to the end of the group. Patients perceived themselves as healthier at the end of the group than they did at the beginning.

Comments from Patients

Patients' responses to GMAs are overwhelmingly positive. We once asked people this open-ended question: "What do you like about group medical appointments?" Here are some of their answers:

- "I don't feel so alone."
- "I liked the friendliness of it all."
- "I always had the feeling I was the only person with health problems."
- "I felt listened to."
- "It gave me the time to remember my questions."
- "I particularly like the input from other patients."
- "It was comfortable."
- "The doctor didn't have to rush to the next patient. I felt I was listened to."
- "The interaction provided answers to several of my questions."
- "I particularly liked the input from other patients; it was great."
- "I was pleased with the doctor's thoroughness."
- "The personal care was great. Thank you."
- "Very related to my problems and supportive of other patients."
- "I appreciate the improved relationship with my physician and nurse."

Table 3.3 New patient satisfaction survey

GMA					
Pre-group survey	*Excellent*	*Very good*	*Good*	*Fair*	*Poor*
Availability of Appt.	33	33	10	2	1
Amount of time with Dr	13	38	24	4	0
Courtesy/Helpfulness	46	23	8	2	0
Explanation	22	38	13	5	1
Personal Manner	40	27	10	2	0
Overall visit	29	33	15	2	0
Total	**183**	**192**	**80**	**17**	**2**
Percentage	36.60	40.50	16.90	3.60	0.40
Perception of Health	8	16	36	15	4
Percentage	10.10	20.30	45.60	19	5
Post group Survey					
Availability of Appt.	55	24	7	0	0
Amount of time with Dr	57	21	7	1	0
Courtesy/Helpfulness	66	16	4	0	0
Explanation	63	15	8	0	0
Personal Manner	71	11	4	0	0
Overall visit	60	21	5	0	0
Total	**372**	**108**	**35**	**1**	**0**
Percentage	72	21	6.80	0.20	0
Perception of Health	20	18	36	8	4
Percentage	23.30	21	42	9%	4.70

Source: Sutter Medical Foundation, Sacramento, CA.

Table 3.4 Pre and post new patient survey on the recommendation of GMAs

Pre-group	*Definitely yes*	*Probably yes*	*Probably no*
	24	48	7
Percentage	30.4	60.8	8.8
Post-group	54	30	2
Percentage	62.8	34.9	2.3

- "I value being with others dealing with similar challenges."
- "I love the education."
- "I value getting the opportunity to ask questions."
- "I enjoy the social environment."

Physician Satisfaction

It is true that GMAs save physicians time and money, but the response we hear most often from physicians is that they simply *enjoy* GMAs more than individual appointments. Greater satisfaction may be the most important benefit to doctors. This satisfaction comes partly from being able to deliver better care, partly because opening up the schedule relieves stress, and partly because they enjoy the new, less formal, and more intimate relationships with patients that GMAs bring them.

"The shared appointments are not only convenient for me, but I find them to be a nice break from the usual grind," says Dr Dan Fields of Sutter Laguna Medical Group in Elk Grove, California. "The patients always leave the group appointment enjoying themselves."

A physician-satisfaction survey was conducted in March 2002 at Sutter Medical Foundation. Fourteen physicians were asked to respond to five narrative questions about their GMAs, 13 of 14 physicians completed the survey. Listed here are the questions asked, with the answers for the questions listed after each.

1. What did you initially want your GMA to accomplish?
    - Better access.
    - Help with complicated patients.
    - Change the dynamics with the doctor–patient interaction so that patients will learn from each other.
    - Psychosocial issues addressed.

- Ability to see a large number of patients in a short period of time.
- A different model for delivery of care.
- Patient education.

2. What has your GMA accomplished?
   - Some help with access.
   - Help with complicated patients.
   - More enjoyment in seeing patients.
   - Lifestyle changes have been easier to enforce and implement.
   - Patients who learn from each other.
   - Mental health access.
3. Did you encounter unexpected benefits?
   - The patients really serve as resources themselves.
   - The patients really love it.
   - I recognize environmental and social contributors to diseases that I would have never noticed.
4. Did you encounter unexpected problems?
   - Difficult to do when I am on call for the office.
   - Office staff are not working well to get the patients into GMAs or to get them checked in and registered when they arrive.
   - Difficult to fill the groups due to scheduling problems.
   - Initial reluctance of patients to attend.
   - Remembering to recommend the group to my patients.
   - Time management.
   - Scheduling the right number of attendees, which has been more or less a thorn in my side.
   - How to handle more than 10 patients and still give each patient the time they need.
5. What unexpected outcomes resulted from your GMAs?
   - Group interaction was good.
   - Relaxation therapy helped.
   - Seeing children in GMAs has been okay.
   - Many of my patients have done so remarkably well with the help of the GMA.
   - Patients really connected with each other and gave each other support.
   - I enjoy my practice more.
   - I can do better patient education, which results in better outcomes.
   - The health of patients has improved.
   - A reduction in the demands on my staff has occurred.
   - I have been helped with limit setting and boundaries.
   - I have met some really great people, and it probably was the catalyst in terms of doing some of my own self-improvement work.
   - It is a relief from the grind.

6. How important is your GMA in your practice?
   - Extremely important: 64%
   - Very important: 28%
   - Moderately important: 7%
   - Not important: 0%

The GMA becomes a tool in the toolbox that benefits everyone—patients, physicians, and staff—as we see in Chapter 4.

Chapter 4

Why It Works: Benefits to Patients

Group medical appointments (GMAs) are the ultimate win–win partnership for doctors and patients. In the groups, no benefit comes to patients without also benefiting physicians and vice versa.

It is somewhat artificial to separate benefits that are for patients from those that are for physicians, but this chapter details the benefits that appear to focus primarily on patients. It then shows how GMAs bring into play all of the therapeutic effects of groups set forth by Irvin Yalom (1995), Emeritus Professor of Psychiatry at Stanford University School of Medicine, in *The Theory and Practice of Group Psychotherapy.*

Patients Can Be Seen More Quickly

Because GMAs meet at least once a week, patients no longer have to wait weeks or months for an appointment. They can call a few days in advance or even on the same day. This quick access minimizes visits to the emergency room, which is the most expensive place to get care.

"It gives me great peace of mind to be able to call my doctor and know that I can see him the very next day," says one patient who has attended a GMA. "It beats having to wait 5 weeks to see my doctor. I really enjoy these appointments."

Patients do not have to wait an hour after they arrive at the office. GMAs happen on time and are not subject to the "schedule slippage" that most medical offices experience.

DOI: 10.4324/9781003673521-5

"Greater access" is one of the primary benefits that both patients and physicians noted.

Patients Get More Time with Their Physician

Patients can spend 90 minutes with their physicians instead of the 10 to 15 minutes normally scheduled for follow-up visits. Their specific medical issue may be addressed for 5 to 10 minutes of that time, but they have another 80 minutes to watch the doctor work with other patients. Not only do they learn from the treatment of other patients, but they also feel as if they know their doctors better because they have seen him or her deal with a variety of situations. People are often better able to make positive changes in their lives by observing the good and bad behaviors and interactions of other patients than if they are confronted directly about their behavior.

This extended, in-depth interaction is more satisfying for both doctors and patients. The setting is relaxed. The doctor is not struggling to get as much information as he or she can, as quickly as possible, in order to deliver treatment and get out the door. Everybody is more at ease, and the pace feels slower than in individual appointments.

Patients Can Be Seen More Frequently

GMAs free physicians' schedules and allow 12 people to be seen at once. This means that physicians can be generous with follow-up visits and have people come in at optimal intervals, rather than "the longest interval they can go without being seen and still be safe."

This greater capacity for frequent visits makes it easier to

- Monitor and fine-tune medications.
- Check in with patients about behavioral changes such as exercise, diet, and blood sugar levels.
- Give more attention to patients who have an emotional or psychological need.
- Continue educational programs such as yoga demonstrations, stress-reducing and relaxation techniques, and breathing and visualization exercises.
- Surface and address underlying psychosocial issues such as addictions, financial trouble, or family problems.
- Get to know patients in more personal ways, which often aids in their diagnosis and treatment and gives physicians greater satisfaction.

- Provide ongoing guidance with lifestyle changes and chronic disease management.
- Manage common psychiatric conditions when psychiatry resources are scarce or difficult to obtain in a timely fashion.

Patients Feel Better About Their Care

When patients can be seen quickly, frequently, and for longer periods of time, they feel better about their care. When patients feel better about their care, they relax. When patients are relaxed, they are easier and more pleasant to be around. They are more cooperative about their treatment and less stressed in their interactions with both the physician and staff. They do not call the office as much, a process that consumes large amounts of staff and physician time. I was doing a presentation on GMAs for the employees of a competitor of Sutter Medical Foundation and asked the participants to tell me what it is they know or understand about GMAs. One woman said,

> Well, I know a lot about GMAs. I have attended several GMAs at Sutter, and I can tell you that they care about you at Sutter. I don't have to wait to get in. I can see my doctor when I want, and when I attend the groups, I get a lot of support and information to assist me with my diabetes.

This statement is often heard as GMA patients report feeling that they get more information, more time, more advice, and a higher quality of care in group appointments. They feel treated as whole human beings, rather than as simply diseases or time slots to be handled as quickly and efficiently as possible. Satisfaction and appreciation replace the frustration that often results from not being able to get an appointment, waiting at the office because the doctor is running late, being rushed during the appointment, and feeling "pushed around" by the health care system.

The Mind–Body Component Enhances Care

> *I could never say in the morning, "I have a headache and cannot do thus and so." Headache or no headache, thus and so had to be done.*
>
> **Eleanor Roosevelt**

During a GMA, a 60-year-old man was discussing his recent negative thallium treadmill test with the physician. Another gentleman in the group piped up rather cynically, "Yeah, I had one of those negative treadmills a week before my heart attack last year." The facilitator immediately asked the second gentleman if he was angered by the false-negative test. There was a long pregnant pause, absolute silence in the group, and the reply was, "No. I guess everybody does their best and nothing's perfect." When the facilitator asked the first gentleman how he felt about the uncertainty, he said, "He's right. Nothing's perfect but we hope for the best." He is still alive and well. The two men left arm in arm after the group, discussing their experiences in detail.

Patients get an entirely new dimension of care with the addition of a facilitator who is also a therapist, psychologist, social worker, or other mental health professional. This component gives them immediate access to professional support in dealing with the behavioral components of their illness and an eye that is looking to their psychological as well as their physical needs. They can also access information on and referrals to a broad range of services that are rarely tapped in individual appointments.

The benefits that result from having a mental health facilitator present include the following:

- Patients are more likely to surface and deal with psychosocial or relational factors that may have been contributing to their illness.
- Some psychological and behavioral issues can be addressed in the GMA itself.
- Better diagnoses and referrals for mental health issues exist. The GMA becomes an excellent resource and screening tool that helps patients discover what other kinds of help they may need and where and how to get it. For most patients, mental health assessment and treatment begin and end in the primary care physician's office. If it does not occur there, it often does not occur at all. The mental health facilitator may be quicker to see the need for a referral to a specialist such as a psychotherapist, psychiatrist, or a community service organization.
- "Guest professionals" are more likely to be brought in. These might include dietitians, yoga and meditation instructors, or health educators.
- Little overlap exists in the training of physicians and mental health providers. Treatment becomes more holistic when patients get access to these services and modalities. After facilitating numerous GMAs with a physician, I have come to appreciate fully the benefits of having a physician beside me as I speak with patients. I have heard that many physicians feel the same

> about their mental health facilitator and often comment to me that they wish their facilitator could attend all appointments with them and work as a team for the treatment of all the patients.

During one GMA, the physician was just finishing up with a patient who had cirrhosis of the liver. The behaviorist asked the patient how he was doing since he had stopped drinking, and he said he was having terrible nightmares. He explained that he had been a sniper in World War II, picking off German officers behind enemy lines. He had married a German woman and had never told her, or anyone else, what he had done.

Another World War II veteran happened to be in the group, and this man told him about some helpful treatment options available through the Veterans Administration. He urged the first man not to try dealing with his problem alone when help was available. A woman in the group advised him to tell his wife. "You and your wife have been married for what? Fifty or sixty years?" she said. "I'm sure she has known all along that something was wrong and will be glad to know about this."

This was just one instance in which underlying psychological factors emerged in the group setting that might have stayed buried for years of individual appointments. When it becomes acceptable—and even expected—to address psychosocial and relational factors, patients feel more comfortable entering this arena.

Patients Can Get Care Specific to Their Needs

Unfortunately, most health care—and mental health care—is restricted to visits with primary physicians. For instance, because of few community resources, it falls on the primary care physicians to treat most depression and anxiety, rather than mental health professionals.

An estimated 60% to 80% of the conditions physicians see in primary care are related to stress or lifestyle. This is a natural place for the co-facilitator to suggest an integrated assessment (biomedical and psychosocial), education (e.g., stress management, coping skills, and lifestyle changes), treatment options, and recommendations.

Because GMAs can be used for screening and referral of psychological conditions, they ensure that people see mental health or other professionals if they need to do so. Patients with specific needs can also be referred to therapy, classes, weight-management programs, or even community volunteer organizations if they are looking for somewhere to contribute and that will help their healing.

"Perception of Health" Improves

Since the human body tends to move in the direction of its expectations—plus or minus—it is important to know that attitudes of confidence and determination are no less a part of the treatment program than medical and science technology.

Norman Cousins

This crucial aspect of healing concerns how much control patients feel over their own treatment and health. "Perception of health" almost always improves markedly in GMAs.

Patients in GMAs simply have access to more information and resources. They enjoy the support of the group and encourage one another in lifestyle changes such as exercise, weight loss, and disease management. They feel empowered to try new things and to do things they thought were impossible before they saw other group members do them. Patients meet other patients who may be worse off than they are. They also see themselves as contributors when they make suggestions that help someone else. One woman who never thought she would be able to return to work is now working full time.

GMA patients also have a more realistic picture of their health because they are more likely to keep the records that physicians ask them to keep (e.g., blood sugars and weight). For instance, patients in one pain GMA were asked to keep a log of their pain for two weeks—recording pain levels from 1 to 10. Patients who had been saying that their pain was "at 8 for the whole week" realized when they looked at the actual logged numbers that pain actually ranged between 4 and 8.

Possibly the largest benefit of perception of health is when patients realize that they can positively affect how they feel or the outcome of their chronic condition. Their perception of control actually reduces many of their symptoms and gives patients energy to participate more fully in their own lives. Tasks or goals that they thought they could no longer do again become possibilities, as other patients can help them see different approaches to meeting their goals.

You gain strength, courage, and confidence by every experience in which you really stop to look fear in the face. You are able to say to yourself, "I lived through this horror. I can take the next thing that comes along."

Eleanor Roosevelt

Patients become Partners in Their Own Care

The relationship between doctors and patients becomes a true partnership in GMAs. Most patients and doctors are relieved to discard the hierarchy and patriarchy and become part of a health team that includes the patient, family members, the physician, the co-facilitator, and often the other group members as well.

Physicians enjoy the opportunity to know their patients better because they can be more creative in their diagnosis, treatment, and education. They also enjoy having patients who are more likely to take more responsibility for their own healing—especially when it comes to making behavioral changes, taking advice that they have resisted before the group, and using such ancillary services as support groups, therapy, and other modalities.

Education Increases Exponentially

Education occurs in many innovative ways during a GMA. First, patients learn from watching the physician educate other patients—both about specific diseases and treatments and about general health. Patients who attend GMAs consistently score higher on general health knowledge and on knowledge about their condition than patients with the same condition who attend only individual appointments.

Second, patients can learn from one another's example, encouragement, advice, and experience, even when their situations appear very different. Third, disease-specific GMAs often feature short, 5-minute talks on topics related to the disease. A group for diabetics, for instance, might hear from a podiatrist on foot health during one visit. The next week, someone from the lab might come to explain how lab tests work, why they are needed, and what is important about getting them done correctly and in a timely fashion. The next week, they might hear from an exercise physiologist. Over time, patients' education builds, and they get quite an extensive training. Even in physician-specific groups, the health recommendations for one condition—stress reduction, exercise, and good nutrition—apply to everyone.

Lifestyle and Behavioral Changes Improve

Human beings, by changing the inner attitudes of their minds, can change the outer aspects of their lives.

William James, U.S. pragmatist philosopher and psychologist (1842–1910)

In doing these groups and observing the patients in the groups interact with each other, I have come to realize that patients will take advice, resource information, constructive criticism, and other advice from other patients better than from any professional who is giving them information. When providers give patients advice, patients listen to it through a screen. While they are listening, thoughts occur such as "they don't know what it's like to live with this" or "they have no idea how busy I am," and "I just do not have the luxury of time to take care of myself in the way they are suggesting." They listen to the information from the provider with a "yes, but" going through their mind. When other patients make suggestions, the information is generally received without any of these thoughts. What other patients say is more credible because they have actual experience to back their comments.

GMAs are powerful tools for helping patients make permanent lifestyle changes such as exercise, diet, stress management, weight loss, job changes, and relationship choices and being more assertive and taking their medications regularly.

Sometimes patients are challenged by other group members to make changes, and this motivates them even more strongly than the doctor or co-facilitator's advice. One physician had been trying for 15 years to get a man to stop smoking. The man had cut down, but not quit. One day during the GMA, an older patient picked up a grocery bag full of medications. He shook it at the first man and said, "If you don't want to have to take all of these medications, throw the cigarettes away!" The first gentleman then stopped smoking.

A few months ago this was again exemplified in a GMA that I was conducting on the East Coast. One of the patients attending the group that day was a nurse who was currently employed at the medical group and had worked for them for 30 years. This woman was being seen for many health problems, and it became quickly apparent that she had a lot of stress in her personal life, was working long hours, and was spending very little time taking care of her health. I assumed because of her background that she would put more credibility in what the provider said than in any of the other patients. It was absolutely amazing. Whenever the physician or I made any suggestions or tried to get her to look at and solve some of her problems, she would cross her arms in front of her, sit back in her seat, and promptly tell us why that was not possible for her. When the physician and I gave up and let the group speak with her, things changed. First, her whole body language changed. When other patients shared with her their experiences, thoughts, and advice, she would uncross her arms and lean forward toward the speaker. She would ask specific questions about how they were exercising, how they found time, and what they did to reduce stress; she never once told the other patients "yes, but." She actually went away from the group with an action plan.

Action Plans Start Working

> *Habit is habit and not to be flung out of the window by any man, but coaxed downstairs a step at a time.*
>
> **Mark Twain, U.S. humorist, novelist, short story author, and wit (1835–1910)**

Patients' action plans for making lifestyle changes are far more likely to be effective when they are developed and monitored in the group. The co-facilitator can help patients develop reasonable, achievable plans for changing behaviors and make sure they have the desire and the means to follow those plans. Patients may leave individual appointments willing and even excited about making changes; however, they often try to do too much or to do it all at once or to do it all alone. They might, for instance, start exercising and dieting at the same time, or they might jump right into 30 minutes a day of exercise when they really need to work up to that level.

When these things happen, they naturally get discouraged. Often, they just quit. When patients can come in more frequently, they can be monitored to see how they are doing with their plans. If the plans are not working, adjustments can be made.

GMAs also offer accountability for action plans. Patients know that they will be returning to the group and reporting on what happened with their plans. This helps some patients keep going when they might otherwise have quit. Patients sometimes even call one another for support during the week. When they succeed, they get reinforcement from the group.

GMA patients are also ahead of the game in making their action plans work because they have watched other group members create and succeed with their plans. They begin to understand the pitfalls and to pick up tips for succeeding.

In addition to all of these advantages, group members have access to coaching from the co-facilitator.

Coaching to Action

> *One's philosophy is not best expressed in words; it is expressed in the choices one makes … and the choices we make are ultimately our responsibility.*
>
> **Eleanor Roosevelt**

Even a little coaching can make an enormous difference when patients start creating action plans for making changes. Coaching also gives patients a chance to see what they are really willing to do.

I have found that patients are only willing to do what they are willing to do. If they are going to walk away with a plan they can really follow, they need a safe environment in which they can tell the truth. For instance, they may not be willing to test blood sugar at first—but when they have logged some "wins" with exercise, they may be ready to move on to testing blood sugar. Here is how such a conversation might sound.

In an individual appointment, the physician might simply tell a patient that he or she needs to get more exercise. The patient would nod, go home, and not exercise, and that would be the end of it. That same patient might be asked in the GMA, "What could you do to be more active?" If the patient does not answer, the facilitator might ask, "None of us takes perfect care of ourselves. What is one thing you are willing to do?"

He or she might say, "Exercise." This response is so vague that if the patient were not asked a follow-up question, the chances of him or her actually exercising would probably be quite low.

"What does that look like?" the facilitator might ask. "What kind of exercise? And how much?"

After that, the facilitator would coach the patient to a realistic plan and make suggestions for implementing it. After they put together the plan, the facilitator might ask, "On a scale of 1 to 10, how confident are you that you will do this?"

If the patient gives any answer of less than 7, he or she probably will not do it. If he or she says "10," the plan may be too easy. The facilitator then coaches the patient to make the plan something that he or she is willing to do—but not so easy that the exercise does not produce the intended result (Box 4.1).

> *In the long run, we shape our lives, and we shape ourselves. The process never ends until we die. And the choices we make are ultimately our own responsibility.*
>
> **Eleanor Roosevelt**

There Is No Failure—Only Winning and Learning

I believe that it is impossible to fail with an action plan. An action plan is objective information. Even when patients do not follow their plans precisely, coaching can help them see what got in the way and what adjustments will help them succeed.

BOX 4.1 GMA ACTION PLAN

ACTION PLAN FOR

(Name) ________________________

Week(s) of ________________________

Goal: ____

I am willing to ____

How much? ____

When? ____

How often? ____

I am telling ___________________________ about my intentions and plan, asking for support if I need it. Log/notes on progress, completion

*You can't fail an action plan. If you did not do it—that's information you can use. If it was too easy—that too is information.

Source: © DeeAnn Schmucker 2006

Sometimes patients with chronic diseases, especially chronic pain, develop a mindset that they cannot succeed. If they have not followed their plan, they may come into the appointment and just look down at the floor when it is their turn to speak. I always tell these patients that they cannot fail with an action plan. They can learn from a plan, but they cannot fail. They can see what they are willing to do and what they are not willing to do. They can learn the extent of their physical and psychological capacities, but they cannot fail.

At the very least, these patients come away with valuable information. If they do not do one particular part of their plan, that is information. The questions simply become these: What got in the way? What will work better? Was that part of the plan even realistic? This kind of coaching is a powerful educational tool—not just for the patient working on the action plan, but also for everyone in the group.

Sometimes it is difficult for patients to predict what will be possible for them in any given week, especially when they have chronic pain. There is no shame in laying out a plan and not being able to follow it. The co-facilitator just guides them to see what did and did not work. He or she helps them make course corrections, own their plans, and cause them to succeed. This is empowering for patients.

After patients have seen one or two of these coaching interactions in the group, everybody gets the idea of how it works. Many patients begin thinking along these "coaching" lines, even when they are away from the group and the co-facilitator is not present to guide them.

Patients in GMAs are far more likely to succeed with their action plans because they are better educated about their condition, they have the co-facilitator's help in developing their plans and making adjustments, they enjoy the built-in support and encouragement from the group, and they have a fail-safe reward in the acknowledgment of other group members.

> *Aim for success, not perfection. Never give up your right to be wrong, because then you will lose the ability to learn new things and move forward with your life. Remember that fear always lurks behind perfectionism. Confronting your fears and allowing yourself the right to be human can, paradoxically, make yourself a happier and more productive person.*
>
> **David M. Burns, MD**

The Group Itself becomes Part of the Healing

The group itself is healing. Group members come to appreciate one another's experience and wisdom. They love to support one another and contribute to one another. Most patients thrive in this environment, even if they have had initial concerns about discussing their situations "with strangers." Those strangers often become some of the strongest members of their support teams—friends in healing who contribute to their success.

Support of the Group

"Group support" is always listed high in surveys of what patients like about GMAs. Most groups foster a tremendous sense of mutual help and contribution. Patients become part of a larger whole in which everyone is working together toward healing. They benefit from the positive, hopeful attitude in the group and see that they are not alone. Sometimes the group is the only place in the patient's life where that kind of support occurs.

Physicians and co-facilitators are often surprised at the treasure trove of wisdom in the group. A newly diagnosed patient might ask a question or voice a concern about some aspect of diabetes, for instance, and another patient might share his or her own experience of the same situation. New patients are often more reassured by what other patients say than they are by the doctor's or co-facilitator's words. People who have actually walked the path on which the new patient is embarking have often discovered solutions that might not occur to the physician or the behaviorist.

People in the group often become active members of one another's health teams. In one group, a man who was quite ill with complications from diabetes got very excited because his estranged wife was letting their teenage daughter come for a 3-week visit that summer. With the support of the group, he went on an intense program of diet, exercise, and medication to improve his health so that he could be more active and enjoy more fully those three weeks—it worked.

At the last minute, however, the wife decided not to let their daughter visit for that length of time, and he only got to see her for one day. He was devastated and became very depressed. At one point, he had to leave the group so that people would not see him cry. The co-facilitator followed him out of the room and convinced him to use the group as a source of comfort and support. He came back in the room and told the group that he felt like going off his program and did not care if he became very ill again. The group came up with several ideas to get him out of his isolation. He wound up taking all of the newly found energy to support other children in the community by volunteering at a neighborhood school. It gave him a new lease on life.

We have seen group members help one another with parenting, grandchildren, single motherhood, and many other issues. Sometimes the support only takes the form of saying, "Yes, I went through that, too." Sometimes, however, that is enough. More often, group members tell one another, "Yes, that happened to me, and this is how it affected my health. This is where you can get support, and this is what you can do to help yourself." People are extraordinarily willing to take advice from other group members, and the group becomes an upward spiral of healing.

> *Of course there is no formula for success except perhaps an unconditional acceptance of life and what it brings.*
>
> **Arthur Rubinstein, U.S. (Polish-born) composer and pianist (1886–1982)**

Learning from Feedback

Patients also learn from the group's feedback. They can often hear and absorb observations from other group members more readily than they can from the doctor or the co-facilitator. In a report that recently crossed my desk, a co-facilitator described a particularly combative man in his twenties:

> The group didn't pull any punches with him, telling him he was being "a jerk," something neither I nor the doctor would have been able to do. He soon learned by the other members' examples that when he framed his responses in a better light, he received a more positive response. Peer pressure is very powerful.

The feedback can be positive as well. At one group, I noticed a young woman with lupus visibly brighten when another woman in the group assured her that she "looked much better than last time."

More Positive Perspective

GMAs can give patients a new perspective on their own illness and suffering, and this often brings relief. One time I was sitting with the physician as patients came into the GMA. He leaned over, pointing out a woman to me, and said she was the sickest patient in his panel. Every one of her organ systems was in trouble, with the exception of her lungs.

This woman happened to sit next to a woman who had asthma. The physician spoke with the asthma patient first. After he was finished addressing that woman's issues, the very sick patient leaned over and told the woman with asthma, "I sure feel sorry for you with that asthma. I'm going away a lucky woman because I don't have asthma."

The Healing Power of Contribution

> *When you cease to make a contribution, you begin to die.*
>
> **Eleanor Roosevelt**

Patients with chronic conditions often feel that they have nothing to offer the world. Nevertheless, when they find themselves sharing valuable information with others in the group, they feel empowered and validated.

One woman in a family practice GMA confessed that her boyfriend was abusing her both emotionally and physically. She said that she wanted him to leave but that he was the father of her baby and she did not think it was fair to her child to separate from him. The physician and co-facilitator were trying to get her to discuss her options, but she did not budge.

Another woman in the group was listening intently. When the first patient stopped speaking, the second woman looked at her and said, "I was in a relationship just like that years ago. Leave this man. If he treats you that way, he is a sperm donor—not a father to your child. There are good men out there. I know. I found one." For the first time during that group, the first patient listened. This interaction was beneficial for both women. One got good advice; the other got the joy of contributing.

When doctor, patient, co-facilitator, and other group members come together to solve problems, everybody makes a contribution, and everybody feels better for it.

Openness to Trying New Things

> *The truth that makes men free is for the most part the truth which men prefer not to hear.*
>
> **Herbert Agar**

Patients in GMAs tend to be more open to trying new things. This works in several ways:

1. *New regimens.* Patients sometimes resist new regimens, such as starting insulin. If other patients who are already on insulin share about their treatment and success, they can have an enormous impact. They have been where the new patients are. They can say that they, too, were reluctant to take that step—but that they did, and it worked for them.
2. *New modalities.* Occasionally, patients resist new holistic modalities such as yoga, visualization, meditation, or even more traditional suggestions such as diet and exercise. Again, they tend to become more open when other group members share their initial hesitation and then go on to talk about the benefits they realized when they tried the new treatment or modality.
3. *Indirect advice can be more acceptable.* Patients can often hear and accept the physician's advice better when it is spoken to *other* people. One woman who had been told to lose weight simply refused to follow the diet the doctor gave her. In the group, she watched him interact with another overweight person and realized how important it was for that person to lose weight. She could extrapolate the conversation to her own situation and immediately started following her diet. She could hear the information

without getting defensive when it was delivered indirectly and spoken to someone other than herself.

4. *Advice from other patients can be more acceptable.* The advice from other patients may not be medical, but sometimes that is not what people need. One patient's mental health issues were being exacerbated by his alcohol abuse, and he was resisting the doctor and therapist's advice to seek help for his alcoholism. Another member in the group, a young woman about his age, shared about Alcoholics Anonymous and the difference that it had made in her life. His demeanor softened, and he started to listen. Sometimes this kind of personal sharing and advice helps more than anything the providers could say.

5. *Peer pressure.* Group members often make beneficial changes as a result of peer pressure in the group. Dr Daniel Berger of Sansum reports, "Some patients would just never monitor their blood glucose levels. Now almost everybody comes with his or her sheets or log books. They are almost embarrassed if they don't have their numbers with them. Other patients who have been helped by the group are those who need to transition to insulin. They are sometimes reluctant, until other patients in the group say, 'I was where you are a year ago, and I didn't want to but I did and it's working.'"

Community

GMAs create community, and this kind of support is almost always an advantage, particularly in the treatment of chronic disease. People with chronic conditions tend to be isolated, and the group provides a perfect community for them. They begin to feel more hopeful when they are part of a group. Time after time, we hear, "I don't feel so alone."

Even patients who initially say that they are not "group people" usually enjoy the sense of community that springs up in GMAs. One patient with chronic pain was very depressed. I had actually done a suicide interview with her and discovered that she had a definite plan to kill herself and the means to carry out that plan. She was estranged from her mother and had no family other than her young daughter. The daughter was the only reason she had not attempted suicide before then. It was right before Thanksgiving, and she was particularly depressed about the upcoming holidays. During the GMA, she got two invitations from other group members to join them and their families for Thanksgiving. After the group, these people got together and exchanged phone numbers so that they could continue supporting her and making plans with her.

Being part of a community helps people feel more positive about their treatment. They usually have more in common with one another than they thought they would and are amazed to hear stories so similar to their own.

Privacy Issues

Most patients' concerns about privacy dissolve quickly in the warmth of the group. They are happy to sacrifice a little privacy for greater access to care, spending more time with the physician, and the sharing, learning, and support they get from the group. (Exams, such as pelvic or prostate exams, that do require some privacy are not done in the group.)

In one group, a patient said she was there to get her labs but that she also had a sore on her bottom and wanted the physician to look at it. He said he would go over the lab work in the group and afterward would take her back to an exam room to look at the sore. She said, "No, just do it now." She walked over to him and pulled her pants down just a little bit in the back so that he could see. He wrote her a prescription, and that was that.

Sometimes the "lack of privacy" turns out to be a benefit. One facilitator reported,

> In one of my groups, we have several women in their 60s and 70s who attend on a semiregular basis. A new participant joined the group and shyly asked the doctor about the urinary leakage she had been experiencing. Three other women in the group admitted that they had the same problem but had been too embarrassed to bring it up. Had this new woman not joined the group that particular day, the others may never have discussed it.

In the easy familiarity of the group, privacy becomes less of an issue than people imagine.

> *People are pretty much alike. It's only that our differences are more susceptible to definition than our similarities.*
>
> **Linda Ellerbee**

We recognized from the beginning that GMAs are not for everyone, and this was also borne out in the survey. Although most patients indicated there was not anything about the group they disliked, some commented as follows: "I don't like talking about my problems in front of other people." "I didn't feel like burdening everyone with more than one problem." "The group was larger than I expected."

Overall, we see positive trends in patients' access, outcomes, and satisfaction with GMAs. Some reasons for this are the addition of a mental health facilitator, greater opportunities for education and using community resources, and more partnering with physicians on their own care. However, the fundamental benefit of simply being in a group with the purpose of promoting healing cannot be overlooked.

Irvin Yalom's 11 Therapeutic Factors of Groups

Irvin Yalom is the father of group psychotherapy. In *The Theory and Practice of Group Psychotherapy* (1995), he describes 11 therapeutic factors that occur in groups. Looking at the specific benefits that Yalom attributes to being part of a group gives some insight into why GMAs produce such positive results.

Here is how each of his 11 positive dynamics shows up in GMAs.

Instillation of Hope

- Research shows that having hope correlates with positive therapeutic outcomes.
- Patients are far more hopeful when they see others in the group coping effectively with similar problems.

Universality

- Many patients believe that their problem is unique, and this attitude is often heightened by social isolation. When they hear other patients discuss similar problems, they feel less isolated and more understood. A sense that everyone is "all in the same boat" begins to emerge.
- Despite the complexity of human problems, no human thought or action is fully outside the experience of other people. Discovering that they have more in common with other patients than they had thought they did often reduces patients' anxiety and sense of urgency about their health problems.

Imparting Information

- Information is power—and stress reduction. Anxiety stemming from uncertainty often creates more havoc than the primary disease. Groups are an excellent opportunity for patients to ask questions and get information. When responses come quickly and easily, they feel that they have gained more control over their lives and become more relaxed about their treatment.

- In groups, patients receive education from a variety of sources. Often the experience of another patient is the best source of education. Patients often listen to and absorb observations from patients more readily than they can from the physician or co-facilitator.
- GMAs are an excellent opportunity to teach patients about the disease process and lifestyle management.
- Physicians can give information to many patients at once, instead of repeating the same information many times over the course of a day, without the time constraints that are a part of individual appointments.

Altruism

- People with chronic conditions often feel a deep sense of having nothing to offer others. Finding out that they are able to help other group members with information and support is refreshing and boosts their sense of self-worth.
- Patients receive through giving.

Corrective Recapitulation of the Primary Family Group

- Observing healthy interactions and participating in them can often serve as a corrective healing experience for patients.
- Patients make changes that help them function more easily and effectively in the world.

Development of Socializing Techniques

- GMAs offer accurate feedback from others and give direction for making changes to function better in the world.
- Groups are a powerful model for healthy behaviors. Patients learn to resolve conflict, to experience giving and receiving accurate empathy, to be less judgmental, and to understand better the areas in which they could benefit from changes.

Imitative Behavior

- Patients see that certain behaviors are positively reinforced, and other behaviors are discouraged. The group is a place to practice new behaviors and new responses.

Interpersonal Learning

- Groups help keep patients focused on the here and now, reducing time spent lamenting lost ability and moving them toward active problem-solving.
- Change can be an emotional and corrective experience. Having other group members respond honestly and spontaneously "holds up the mirror" for patients so that they can see the impact of their behavior.

Group Cohesiveness

- Patients quickly develop group cohesiveness and a sense of solidarity. The level of this cohesiveness varies, but it is always present.
- Cohesiveness helps patients be more accepting and understanding of one another.
- Patients feel safe enough to be vulnerable with one another.

Catharsis

- The opportunity to purge feelings often gives patients room to look at their current unhealthy behavior and to adopt healthier behavior.
- In GMAs, patients are more likely to tell the truth, take responsibility, and be accountable to the other group members.

Existential Factors

- Patients see and are more likely to accept the fact that life is sometimes unfair and unjust. This can help them get "unstuck" from regret and self-pity and deal more proactively with "what is."
- They recognize that ultimately there is no escape from some of life's pain or from death.
- They understand that no matter how close they get to other people, they must still face life alone.
- When patients face the basic issues of life and death, and as a result start living life more honestly, they are less likely to get caught up in trivialities.

- They learn that they must take ultimate responsibility for the way they live their lives, no matter how much guidance and support they get from others.

All of the benefits to patients discussed in this chapter also benefit physicians. When patients get what they need, physicians know that they are doing their job. When patients are happy about their care, interacting with them becomes more satisfying and pleasant.

Similarly, patients get even better care from happier, more satisfied physicians who are enjoying the benefits described in the next chapter.

Chapter 5

What You Get: Benefits to Physicians

As much as group medical appointments (GMAs) benefit patients, they may benefit physicians even more. Life gets easier and better for physicians whenever patients experience increased access, outcomes, and satisfaction. Additional benefits to physicians range from financial advantages to saving time and energy, to delivering more and better care, to practicing the kind of medicine that first drew them to the profession.

GMAs offer doctors a way to practice medicine with care, compassion, and creativity. Because many experience less stress and more fulfillment, they are less likely to burn out. "I feel good about what I've done at the end of the day," said one doctor.

Physicians say that human values—more personal and holistic care and more relaxed and equal relationships with patients—are even more important to them than the savings in time, money, and energy that they experience with GMAs. In fact, physicians almost always report that they enjoy GMAs more than they do individual appointments and look forward to the days when GMAs are scheduled. They get more done. They enjoy patients more, and they get greater control over their schedules—which means that they are better able to manage large panels of patients.

Each section in this chapter focuses on a specific benefit that physicians realize from GMAs.

 DOI: 10.4324/9781003673521-6

Physicians Can See More Patients without Sacrificing Quality of Care

It has become appallingly obvious that our technology has exceeded our humanity.

Albert Einstein (1879–1955)

The bottom line is that GMAs let physicians see more people per hour without working any harder—and actually deliver a higher quality of care. GMAs often relieve a physician's burden in one area of their practice so that they can focus on other areas that need attention. For example, a physician may be experiencing a backlog in appointments typically thought of as being only individual appointments, such as seeing new patients, physicals, or consults. The physician can design a group to deal specifically with one of those visit types or can create groups for follow-up appointments to free time in their schedule for those longer, more complicated visits such as consults.

Typically, follow-up visits are scheduled every 15 minutes, but every physician knows that some patients only require 10 minutes, whereas others require 45 minutes or more. A day based on 15-minute appointments quickly gets out of control. To make matters worse, many physicians block out certain hours—for example, from 11:00 to 1:00—for paperwork and lunch. If each morning appointment takes 30 minutes, however, physicians do not eat lunch, and they do not get the paperwork done. Paperwork is added to the end of the day, and the scheduling problem snowballs.

One rheumatologist, Dr JaNahn Scalapino, was feeling tremendous time pressure a few years ago when her partner left the practice. She seized on GMAs as a way to see 12 patients in the same time that it normally took her to see 6. She told me that she would have been tearing her hair out without the groups. It was a way to see everyone that she needed without going crazy.

Not only can physicians see more patients in any given time period, but they can also give patients more access and a higher quality of care, using existing resources. They come away knowing that they have done their best for patients and have given them more than they could ever have given in individual appointments. That creates a lot of satisfaction.

Time Is Used More Productively

GMAs allow physicians to use their time more productively in several ways:

1. *Seeing 12 patients at once obviously eliminates all the time wasted in switching from one exam room to the next and in conversational "start-up time"—the small talk and personal questions that establish a connection with each new patient.* Some physicians report that they spend as much time on the physical logistics of moving from room to room and reconnecting with each patient as they do actually practicing medicine.
2. *Physicians can complete required data collection and charting during the appointment instead of having to set aside special times for these activities.* While patients are interacting with the facilitator or other patients, the physician can often complete these entries.
3. *Physicians do not have to repeat information individually for each patient.* When they speak to the group of patients with diabetes about diet and exercise, for example, everybody hears the message at the same time. Questions can also be answered once instead of 12 times. Because GMA patients naturally become better educated about their conditions, physicians can speak to them in more depth.
4. *The workload is decreased so that physicians can spend their time more productively, doing things that only they can do.*
5. *Interruptions are minimized.* The GMA is sacrosanct time. Nobody bothers the physician for phone calls, salespeople, pharmacy calls, signatures, general inquiries, or any of the numerous interruptions normally experienced in the course of a day. In a normal day, sometimes things get so hectic that even seeing patients may seem like an interruption. This is understandable in a system that requires physicians to run from appointment to appointment, re-creating their relationship with each patient, getting information, examining the patient, and delivering care every 15 minutes. With GMAs, physicians get 90 relaxed, uninterrupted minutes with patients. They can be more at ease, and patients feel more important.
6. *The patients help provide the treatment in the support and advice they give.*

GMAs Are Highly Cost-Effective

Physicians are under tremendous pressure to deliver more care in less time for less money. Very few additional resources are needed to start GMAs—a room, some leadership, and some staff education—and the savings in both hard and soft costs are significant.

GMAs are reimbursed in exactly the same way as individual appointments, as you are billing for the medical care delivered. Just as in individual appointments, the progress note must match the billing code used. This means that although physicians spend less time and energy and actually provide more complete care, it is easy to leverage their time by at least 200%.

There are further savings in soft costs. Patients who attend GMAs tend to be less anxious and thus have less need for "phone time" with physicians and staff. Time is saved that would otherwise be spent in staff taking notes from the patients, consulting doctors, and then either staff or doctors calling patients back. Any time that is spent attending to patients outside of actual appointments is reduced with GMAs. Other soft costs include the reduction of HbA1cs, LDLs, blood pressure, and pain medication.

What is the cost of perception? In professional journals, at conferences, and in our own conversations with our colleagues in our organizations, high patient satisfaction has been found to be vital to fiscal solvency. We spend a significant amount of time and money trying to figure out how to increase patient satisfaction. Studies on patient satisfaction show that patients are as satisfied, or in most cases more satisfied, with their experience in GMAs over individual appointments.

Patients tend to use the groups more often at first, and later, when they have more control over their chronic condition, they make fewer visits than before they had attended the group.

Physicians Can Adopt an Attitude of Abundance

GMAs let physicians work from abundance, rather than scarcity. The attempt to use resources wisely sometimes produces a feeling that everything—time, money, people, care—is scarce. Being "penny wise and pound foolish" can backfire. We know that by limiting care we actually increase the demand for care. When patients feel as if they might not be able to get what they need, they become anxious and are more likely to insist on getting everything they need—*now*.

GMAs allow both physicians and their patients to adopt an attitude of abundance. There is enough time, enough energy, and enough resources for patients to get what they need and for both doctor and patient to feel good about the care that is being given.

Doctors no longer have to wonder how long they can safely go before rescheduling patients. In the abundant environment of GMAs, the physician can ask, "What is optimal? What will produce the best care possible?" If the patient should really come back in one or two weeks, instead of three months, there is no problem with scheduling. If a depression patient needs to be seen earlier than the usual six months in order to adjust medications for effectiveness and side effects, there is room in the schedule. He or she can simply attend a GMA.

There is also enough "doctor" to go around. The doctor has enough time and energy to see everyone who needs to be seen without racing from patient to patient delivering instant care that may or may not meet patients' needs.

This attitude of abundance spreads to staff. Dr Berger of Sansum says,

> Our staff enjoys the GMAs and looks forward to them. GMAs are more efficient, and our staff [members] feel as if they can give our patients more. They can get patients in when they need to be seen. The staff even takes notes while I'm consulting with patients, and so everybody gets a summary sheet of their appointment to take away with them.

Mental Health Facilitators Make Care Easier and More Comprehensive

Physicians recognize almost immediately that they have an important ally in the professional who co-facilitates the GMA. Appointments are easier when someone is helping to manage the group's energy and time, keeping people on track, and making sure to unearth any underlying psychosocial issues. Mental health facilitators are also available for questions about and referrals to various holistic modalities and to community and mental health resources.

This additional perspective and expertise make care flow more smoothly and effectively. Sometimes this support is just a matter of asking one timely question. One facilitator told me,

> I had a woman in a group who was having a hard time sleeping. I asked her if this could be because she was afraid she'd never wake up. She had to admit that was the reason. The doctor later told me he would have never thought to have asked that.

Mental health professionals are also able to coach patients on their action plans, facilitate communication between doctor and patient if necessary, and share the management of more complicated or needy patients. When I was setting up GMAs at Sutter, my staff of therapists, most of whom were also trained in other alternative treatment modalities, were often asked to share their expertise in ways that included yoga demonstrations for chronic pain, stress-reducing and relaxation techniques, and breathing and visualization exercises.

Sometimes the help that facilitators provide is very "hands on." One GMA patient was having difficulty dealing with her lower back pain. The physician asked whether she was doing the exercises that she had been given on the last visit. The patient said, "Not always," which we know means "no." The physician then asked whether the patient knew where those exercise sheets were. The patient said, "I'm not sure," again which meant "no."

All of this meant that the patient had no idea where to begin with the exercises. The physician handed her another sheet of exercises, assuming that this would solve the problem. I had been watching this interaction and had a sense that the patient still did not understand how to do the exercises. What we at this point had offered the patient had been offered before. Thus, we were providing the patient with the same plan, but expected different results. The definition of insanity has been described as doing something the same way every time and expecting different results. I decided we needed to do something different to get the different result we were hoping for. I offered to demonstrate them, but the physician said that she wanted to do it. Thus, she got down on the floor and did a pelvic tilt. I still saw some confusion on the patient's face, even though she was saying that she understood. I asked the patient whether she would be willing to get down on the floor with the physician and try the exercise. The patient got down on the floor, but could not figure out how to do the pelvic tilt until the physician actually helped move her through it. She was then able to do it. The patient went away with a smile on her face, knowing what to do.

The physician did the work, but the job of the mental health facilitator in this case was to make sure that the doctor and patient understood one another and that the patient got what she needed.

Relationships with Patients Improve

One of the greatest benefits that GMAs offer physicians is a richer relationship with their patients. Over the years we have redesigned scheduling and other elements of medical practice, but these changes did not substantially alter the relationship between patient and physician.

GMAs foster a new partnership between doctor and patient, which improves the relationship in many ways, including the following:

1. *Patients relax when they are seen and treated as equals.* Feeling that they are "less than," or in an inferior position to doctors, increases patients' anxiety. They work against this inferior relationship and in individual appointments often attempt to gain equal footing by asking the doctor personal questions: "How are you? How is the family?"

These efforts usually backfire. Physicians need to work quickly—greeting, gathering information, answering questions, and delivering treatment, all in 10 to 15 minutes. They sometimes see these kinds of questions as time-consuming obstacles to doing what needs to be done—all of which makes them feel even more rushed and often makes physicians seem brusque.

Patients want more time, more attention, and more equality. Doctors are trying to treat the disease and get on to the next appointment, for which they are already late. The appointment can easily become a contest between doctor and patient—a struggle for focus with the doctor pushing for diagnosis and treatment and the patient pushing for equality and attention.

One study showed that in 15-minute individual appointments, patients had the perception that they had received 5 to 7 minutes of the physicians' time, and physicians felt as if they had given 25 minutes. In GMAs, each patient felt as if he or she had received 90 minutes of attention, and physicians felt as if they had given each patient 5 to 10 minutes. Over the years, the practice and delivery of medicine have gone through great changes with both providers and staff being asked to work harder and harder. What is it that the patients see out of our efforts? Nothing—that is, nothing positive anyway. The changes that patients have seen are longer waits, less time, less relational connection with their provider, a decrease in access, and more cost.

GMAs bring relief to both physicians and patients by placing them on more equal footing. They transform the adversarial relationship into a partnership that is rare when patients are only seen in individual appointments. This is a significant and positive change.

2. *Relationships need not be constantly jump-started.* Physicians spend a great deal of time jump-starting relationships with patients. It begins the minute the doctor walks through the door to the exam room. Almost always, he or she is late and has to begin the appointment with an apology. Then the personal connection is established through small talk and questions. Even under the best of circumstances, there are social niceties to be observed. Only then can doctor and patient get down to the issues at hand. When this connection can be made once, rather than 12 times, in the course of 90 minutes, there is more time and energy to deepen the relationship in other ways.

Even after the connection is established in individual appointments, it is tenuous. When the physician looks down at the patient's chart, eye contact is broken—often so is the connection. When patients feel a loss of contact, they may try to remedy the situation by being more assertive, turning the conversation back to personal matters, or in some other way trying to get the physician's attention. The tug-of-war is on, with the patient wanting personal contact and the physician feeling even more rushed and pressured.

The other challenge that often occurs in the time-limited individual appointment is the decision over what is discussed in the allotted time. The provider is primarily concerned with indicators that show new or advancement of disease. They are concerned about things that may put the patient's life at risk. Patients are concerned about what is bothering them the most. They are concerned about the rash, the headache, and the pain. Both the provider and patient need answers to their respective questions.

In GMAs, physicians can look down without patients feeling abandoned because the facilitator and other group members are looking at the patient and listening attentively. When patients know that they have the full attention of the facilitator, as well as other group members, they sometimes do not even notice that the physician is looking away.

Under these conditions, physicians can often complete their charting during the appointment. If they use paper charts, they can take notes. If they use electronic records, they can bring a laptop. Often, templates can be created for the electronic record, which expedites the writing of the note without compromising quality. This represents another savings of time for physicians. (A laptop is the best because the physician can use it while still facing patients. With a desktop, the physician usually has to turn his or her back, and this can make patients feel that he or she is not listening. Dictation is difficult to do in the group, and thus, extra time should be left at the end of the group if the physician uses dictation.)

3. *Getting to know patients better improves care.* In GMAs, doctors usually learn more about their patients' lives than they do in individual appointments—and patients often learn more about their doctors. For instance, the doctor can share once, rather than 12 times, that she is a new grandmother. The result is that she is more likely to do so.

Patients often bring issues in the group that they have not felt comfortable addressing in individual appointments—either because of time pressure or because subjects such as prostate or menopause problems, depression, or anxiety simply did not come up. When other people in the group bring them up, however, a door opens.

When physicians have a fuller picture of the patient's situation, they can offer better and more complete treatment. In the give-and-take of the GMA, where psychological and behavioral issues are included in the discussion, this kind of information emerges naturally to "flesh out" the patient's condition.

One woman in a diabetic group that I facilitated cracked a lot of jokes and was friendly and outgoing with the other patients before the group started. The physician began the group with a patient who was more on the quiet side, and part of the discussion centered on depression. We then continued around the group and finally got to the patient who had seemed so light-hearted. The physician looked at her latest HbA1c and found that it had gone up. He started to address this with her by discussing her medications, but she interrupted him and said, "I, too, am having a lot of depression and anxiety."

The physician and I were very surprised. She went on to say that her son was getting out of jail the next day. She and her husband had had a restraining order against him before he went to prison, but they knew the son was expecting that all would be forgiven when he was released and that he would be coming back to live with them. The other patients in the group told her about several community resources that she could use to deal with this situation and even gave her phone numbers. The physician and the patient decided not to change medications and to reevaluate her condition at the next appointment after the situation with her son had been resolved.

4. *GMAs are great for patients who are difficult or needy.* I often suggest that physicians schedule difficult patients or patients who they do not enjoy seeing as much in GMAs. This gives the physician some "buffer," or distance. There are other people around, and in the relaxed atmosphere of the group, physicians often find that they can appreciate these patients more.

Another part of the equation is that these patients often calm down and become easier to deal with in GMAs. They are not as anxious or needy and actually become contributors to the group.

One administrator says that before they started GMAs, certain patients used to call again and again to see whether they could be seen immediately—they could rarely be seen immediately simply because not enough slots were available in the schedule. She called these patients "frequent flyers." The more frustrated they got, the more they called—the more they called, the more frustrated and irritated the staff got with them. When her medical group began a GMA, these patients could get in and their frustration subsided. The staff was happy because they had something to give these patients. They could offer solutions rather than simply dealing with frustration. Everybody felt better, and staff time could be used in more productive ways.

5. *More satisfied and better educated patients make practicing medicine more pleasant.* It is simply easier and more pleasant to be around patients who are well educated about their disease, pleased with their access and outcomes, enjoy the support of the group, and are free from the anxiety of unanswered questions about their care. These patients are more appreciative of

their physicians and are more relaxed around them. They feel as if they are getting more for their health care dollar—because they are!

This more equal, informal partnership with patients is new territory. Initially, some physicians are concerned that the new relationship means giving away power. They usually find that just the opposite is true. In creating a more equal partnership with patients, they gain freedom. They can practice medicine more easily and more fully—best of all, they enjoy their patients much more. What looked as if it might be a weakness turns out to be a strength.

Physicians Enjoy the Practice of Medicine

It is true that GMAs save physicians time and money, but the response we hear most often from physicians is that they simply *enjoy* GMAs more than individual appointments. Greater satisfaction may be the most important benefit to doctors. This satisfaction comes partly from being able to deliver better care, partly because opening up the schedule relieves stress, and partly because they enjoy the new, less formal, and more intimate relationships with patients that GMAs bring.

"The shared appointments are not only convenient for me, but I find them to be a nice break from the usual grind," says Dr Dan Fields of Sutter Laguna Medical Group in Elk Grove, California. "The patients always leave the group appointment enjoying themselves." Listed here are common experiences described by physicians who have GMAs as one of their practice tools.

- "I have learned more about my patients in one GMA than in all of the prior interactions I have had with them in individual visits."
- "I was better able to handle complicated patients."
- "I enjoyed seeing patients more."
- "Lifestyle changes were easier to implement and enforce."
- "The patients love it! They seem to enjoy sharing and really help each other. Sometimes they even exchange phone numbers and exercise together or end up supporting each other in some fashion."
- "I recognized environmental and social contributors to disease that I wouldn't have otherwise."
- "The patients really serve as resources themselves."
- "I love doing groups. I was ready to quit medicine because of the treadmill I felt like I was on until I began doing groups. I now feel like I can practice the medicine I envisioned in my training."

- "This is the best way to see those chronic patients who need a lot of attention and take a lot of time."
- "I look forward to it! It's a great change from my regular daily routine."

"GMAs are just fun!" says Dr Berger of Sansum. "In some ways, it's like being a talk show host. When I come through the door, I feel like Johnny Carson opening the curtain."

Every health care delivery model has obstacles, and GMAs are no exception. Some obstacles that doctors mentioned included the following:

- "The patients are initially reluctant to attend."
- "Managing time while addressing the group needs is difficult."

Sometimes, however, staff members see things that escape physicians. I once asked a group of physicians whether GMAs had made any changes in the way they practiced medicine or interacted with patients. Some physicians said no, but their staff members later told me that these doctors had become more personable and that patients had noticed this as well.

The bottom line is this: GMAs deliver more and better care per physician hour in a way that is both cost-effective and more satisfying for both physicians and patients. They increase the time patients and physicians spend together without increasing the cost or making further demands on physicians' time or energy. They make psychological, social, and educational support as accessible as medical treatment, and everyone has more fun.

FIRST STEPS

II

A Guide to Setting Up Your Group Medical Appointments

Part II takes you step by step through implementing group medical appointments, making them a productive part of your practice, collecting outcome data, and using ongoing marketing to maintain a high census.

DOI: 10.4324/9781003673521-7

Chapter 6

Preparation: Laying the Groundwork

The successful launch of your group medical appointment (GMA) depends heavily on two factors:

1. Careful, thorough preparation.
2. Your willingness to try something new and possibly change the way you relate to your patients.

This chapter takes you step by step through laying the groundwork for a GMA that serves both your practice and your patients.

Is It Right for You?

Before you launch your GMA, take some time to consider carefully whether this tool is appropriate for your practice—and if it is, how best to shape it for your particular situation.

Here are some questions to ask yourself:

1. What is the most pressing problem in my practice?
2. What do I believe a GMA will do to solve this challenge?
3. What would I *like* my GMA to do to solve this challenge?
4. What would need to happen for this problem to be solved?

DOI: 10.4324/9781003673521-8

5. Is there a particular segment of my patient panel that I want to target?
6. Are there enough of these patients to fill one GMA per week? Two?
7. What resources do I have available (staff, physical facilities, funding)?

GMAs work best for practices that want to give patients more access or that have large numbers of patients who

- Have chronic illnesses or conditions that require regular follow-up care.
- Might benefit from having the emotional and psychosocial aspects of their condition addressed or from receiving ongoing education about their condition.
- Have high emotional needs, require more time with physicians, or need to be seen frequently.

If you have a small practice with no access problems or if your patients do not fall into these groups, GMAs may not be right for you. If your patients do fall into these categories, look at how GMAs could best serve their needs.

"My advice is 'do it!'" says Paul Jaconette, chief administrative officer at Sansum in Santa Barbara, California. "There were initially some concerns about how we would bill for it, and how patients would react—but we have not seen any of the problems we thought might come up. It's been positive for us and for our patients."

It is important early on to get the team (nurses, facilitator, scheduler, administration, and provider) together to plan the group. The structure and the flow of the group need to be mapped out, and tasks need to be delegated and completed. Box 6.1 is a checklist of some of the decisions that need to be made and tasks that need to be completed.

Designing Your Group

After you have decided to go forward, you will need to design your GMA to meet the most pressing needs in your practice. The following questions will help design your group.

BOX 6.1 GMA CHECKLIST

Task	*Responsible Person*	*Due Date*	*Task Completed*
Start Date for Gma Is ______________			
Marketing Posters			
Letters			
Flyers			
Scheduling Change schedule to accommodate group participants			
Review scheduling scripts with schedulers			
Develop strategies for enrolling patients in group			
Locate space, equipment, and staff to do vitals			
Group Room Locate and secure space for group 15+ people			
Put supplies (name tags, pens, paper…) in group room			
Design flow and structure of the Group			
Choose the appropriate staff needed to support the group.			
Verbally review group flow with Staff after details have been determined			
Go over various roles for physician and staff during group.			
Other items			

Source: © **DeeAnn Schmucker 2006**

- Will your GMA be physician specific, disease specific, or a combination?
- Will it include the same patients every time, or can patients drop in? If they can drop in, how much notice must they give that they will be attending—if any?
- How often will the group meet? For groups in which the patients are different every time, I suggest that GMAs meet at least once a week so that they become part of regular office operations. If they meet any less frequently than this, it becomes difficult for patients, physicians, and staff to get into the routine of using GMAs. We find that actually doing GMAs two or more times a week is even better because it becomes a regular tool in your practice. Less than this, it is sometimes easy to forget.
- Will you have a facilitator? Will your facilitator be a mental health professional? Health educator? Nurse? Remember to consider the staff members that are currently working with you as potential facilitators. Each group takes an additional 30 minutes (15 minutes before the group and 15 after) for the facilitator. If staff members are not available, physicians often hire a private-practice mental health professional to come in just for the GMA and pay him or her per group.
- Where will you meet? Do you have access to a room that is large enough to conduct a GMA?
- When will the group be scheduled? What day of the week? What time? The answers to these questions generally depend on your targeted patient population. Working people generally like early groups, late groups, or groups that they can attend over their lunch hour. Older people typically like to avoid rush hour. Another consideration is what time works well for the provider and staff of the clinic. Sometimes the time of group is set by the availability of the space where the group will be held. If the provider plans on having more than one group per week, it is good to pick a time for the second group that may serve a different group of people than the time set for the first group. For example, you may have three groups per week. Monday's group would be from 9:30 to 11:00 a.m., Wednesday's group from 7:30 to 8:30 a.m., and Friday's group from 3:00 to 5:00 p.m.

What You Need to Get Started

"You need a champion," says Dr Daniel Berger of Sansum.

> It's a change for both patients and staff, so you need someone with good organizational skills, and a lot of love and enthusiasm, to get the program up and running. You have to be flexible. You have to make it fun, and you have to want it to succeed.

The champion is usually a physician. Whoever champions your GMA must understand the basics of how GMAs work and how they can help the practice. This person must also bring education and enthusiasm to the rest of the team, be willing to partner with patients, communicate effectively with patients and staff, and be the "buck stops here" person who is responsible for the GMA's success.

"Change is hard," says one administrator. "Physicians need to be enthusiastic, and the staff needs to be educated so that they see all the benefits of GMAs. If the staff isn't enthusiastic, patients won't have the courage to try it."

Secure Support from Administration

Small practices get to skip this section. Large organizations, however, need administrative support. Schedule a meeting with the administrative team, and invite physicians who might be interested in using GMAs to attend. Your presentation to them should include the following:

- Resources currently available within the organization to set up GMAs.
- Data on current finances, access, and disease outcomes. It is important to have these baseline data available to assist in making decisions about current available resources and to determine success at the end of the pilot phase.
- Data on how you anticipate GMAs will affect finances, access, and disease outcomes. Initially, what this applies to is leveraging the physician's time by at least 200%. Disease outcome measurement should start in the first few groups. Often with today's databases, HalC, blood pressure, narcotic use, and lipids are some of the items that are easy to measure.
- Your suggestions for a GMA design that addresses the goals people want to achieve in this practice. For this section, get input from all levels of the staff.
- What resources are needed in terms of funding, support staff, facilities, and promotion?

Enlist a Project Manager

The project manager guides the GMA through its initial stages, establishing a rationale for the GMA and facilitating its implementation within a large organization. He or she identifies physicians with patient panels suitable for the program and provides training to staff and physicians about this new model.

In choosing your project manager, consider these minimal requirements:

- Prior project management or management experience.
- Prior clinical program management and development.
- An understanding of group dynamics.
- Understanding of chronic disease management.
- Prior experience in multidisciplinary teams and team development.
- Excellent communication and conflict resolution skills.
- Individual and group therapy experience.
- Computer skills: word processing, spreadsheets, databases, and email.
- Supervisory experience.

These are the responsibilities your project manager should be prepared to assume:

- Help identify physicians to participate in the GMA program.
- Meet with the physician to design the GMA (i.e., length of time, goals, and types of patients).
- Identify all of the personnel involved with starting and maintaining the GMA.
- Spend time with staff to describe the GMA and answer questions.
- Introduce the facilitator to staff and physician.
- Go over GMA job descriptions with all applicable positions.
- Collaborate with marketing to promote the group (i.e., posters, flyers, brochures).
- Locate space to hold the group that includes the following features: large enough to hold a minimum of 20 people, private space for vitals and more involved examinations, access to restroom facilities, good lighting, good ventilation, and easy patient access.
- Contact physicians weekly to monitor scheduling and answer questions (this discontinues after three to four months, and then contact physician as appropriate).
- Track the number of participants signed up for each group and the number that actually attends.
- Motivate physicians to ensure attendance goals are met (average of 10 to 12 patients for GMAs).
- Orient pertinent staff to documentation, scheduling, and billing procedures.
- Do the many tasks needed to supervise facilitators and other positions specifically assigned to this program.

- Do outcome studies as determined by organizational needs, and share the results with all levels in the organization. It is just as important for the front-line staff as it is for senior management to see these results.
- Give senior management regular updates on program progress.
- Be flexible. Anything can happen!

In addition to making sure that the GMA has adequate infrastructure and ongoing organizational support, the project manager is an ambassador for the GMA—ensuring that everyone involved is clear about the benefits to both patients and physicians.

Often the project manager is someone already in clinical administration (i.e., medical director, nurse manager, access director, and business director). These duties are added to their responsibilities. Generally, this falls in line or complements other responsibilities that the person has. If the organization has plans to offer this throughout their company, then it may be necessary to hire someone to manage it.

It is important that time be provided specifically for GMAs if the project manager is responsible for other projects. This is a large shift in thought, and it takes some monitoring and exploration. Compensation for this position is easily attained when the physician groups are leveraged.

Create Your Plan

Next, create a consolidated business plan of resources (Box 6.2). This plan tells you what you have and what you need. It includes the following:

1. Staff resources
    a. What resources are in place?
    b. What resources, if any, will need to be hired or contracted?
2. Monetary resources
    a. What funds will be required to run the GMA?
    b. What GMA census will be required in order to maintain financial productivity?
3. Start date of group
4. A timeline for tasks that includes the following:
    a. Developing and producing marketing materials.
    b. Charting and scheduling mechanisms in place.
    c. Space located.
    d. Training for team and physicians.
    e. Outcome studies planned and ready to implement.

Recruit Your Team

This team plays a crucial role in starting up your GMA. Each team member needs to pay close attention to detail throughout the planning and implementation process and also to stay flexible in the face of change. With careful planning and a few deep breaths, GMA team members almost always discover that the start-up process is surprisingly simple, professionally rewarding, and highly productive.

BOX 6.2 EXAMPLE OF A BUSINESS PLAN FOR GROUP MEDICAL APPOINTMENTS

Some organizations choose to develop a business plan before proceeding with group medical appointments. A typical business plan defines the scope of work to be undertaken, the resources required to implement the plan, and the expected benefits including return on investment calculations. The following information is included to assist those organizations that choose to create a detailed financial model before starting GMAs.

Start-Up Costs

Here are some of the start-up costs that may be incurred. These are one-time costs to get GMAs started in an organization.

- *Recruiting costs to hire a behaviorist facilitator* If the facilitator is not currently employed in the organization, there will be advertising, interviewing time, and other recruiting costs.
- *Consulting and training* Costs to bring in outside resources to guide the implementation process. Training includes the project manager, physician, facilitator, medical assistant, and schedulers.
- *Marketing* Cost of posters, flyers, mailers, newsletters, etc.
- *Group room space* Cost of identifying and preparing the space to hold groups. Existing space may need renovation to create a comfortable environment for groups. Or, additional space may need to be leased and improved.
- *Group room equipment* Medical equipment like scales, blood pressure cuffs, glucometers, pulse oximeters or spirometers may be needed. Comfortable chairs and tables may need to be purchased. Computer equipment may be needed to connect to practice management and electronic medical record applications.

Ongoing Costs

Here are some of the continuing costs to operate GMAs.

- Facilitator salary, benefits, and training
- Marketing flyers, mailers, newsletters
- Group room space such as lease costs

Return on Investment Calculation

In general, return on investment (ROI) is calculated like this:

$$\text{ROI} = \frac{\text{Start-Up Costs}}{\text{Revenue Increase} - \text{Ongoing Costs}}$$

We've already calculated start-up costs and ongoing costs. Now we need to calculate the revenue increase to complete the formula. This calculation can be as simple or as complex as your organization demands. You may choose to take into account the insurance mix of patients, which affects the actual amount collected. Or, you may simply look at gross billed charges.

Calculating the Revenue Increase from GMAs

The key to calculating the revenue increase is to begin with an agreed-upon measure for the value of a physician's time. You may already have a measure or can easily calculate one. Here are some of the measures that are commonly used:

- Charges per hour
- RVU's per hour
- Encounters per hour

As an example, let's say that our physician generates an average of \$16,000 in charges per week for 40 hours of work (before adding GMAs). So the physician generates \$16,000 Ö 40 = \$400 in charges per hour.

Now, in a 90-minute group medical appointment we estimate the physician will generate \$960 in charges.

The calculation of revenue increase from GMA's goes like this:

GMA charges – (charges per hour × 1.5 hours) or

\$960 – (\$400 × 1.5) = \$960 - \$600 = \$360 per GMA

If we assume two GMAs per week for the physician, the annual revenue increase is:

2 GMAs × 52 weeks × \$360 per GMA = \$37,440 annual revenue increase

Example ROI Calculation

We now have all the numbers for our ROI calculation. So let's go through a simple example. Let's assume that we had \$10,000 in start-up costs and our ongoing costs are \$20,000 per year.

$$\text{ROI} = \frac{\text{Start-Up Costs}}{\text{Revenue Increase} - \text{Ongoing Costs}}$$

$$0.57 = \frac{\$10{,}000}{\$37{,}440 - \$20{,}000}$$

In this example we get a return on our investment in about 7 (.57 × 12) months.

You already have your project manager in place, and Chapter 2 gave you a good idea of what will be expected of other GMA team members. For staff recruitment purposes, you may want to post the following minimum position requirements and responsibilities.

Physician Role

Minimum Position Requirements

- Apply and be chosen to participate.
- Be open and flexible—most importantly, be willing to learn new ways of relating to patients.

Responsibilities

- Market the GMA to both patients and staff (the physician, scheduler, and nurse/medical assistant are responsible for keeping groups full).
- Encourage patients to make their next appointment in the GMA.
- Initially, the physician works closely with the project manager to create a group that meets the specific needs of the practice.
- Develop a relationship with the co-facilitator, and have this person spend a day observing the office practice.
- Plan your day and your schedule to ensure that you arrive at group on time.
- Be open to feedback, and be willing to try new suggestions.
- Meet with the facilitator after each group to debrief.
- Be flexible. Anything can happen!

Facilitator Role

Minimum Position Requirements

- Education: MSW (LCSW or PhD in psychology preferred), RN, or other health professional.
- Extensive experience with chronic disease management. Know the signs and symptoms, diagnosis and treatment options, and specifically the psychosocial issues associated with chronic disease.
- Documented group facilitator experience.
- Documented experience on multidisciplinary teams.
- Ability to work autonomously.
- Ability to use the following computer functions: email, word processing, and spreadsheets.
- Prior experience in partnering with physicians is a plus.

Responsibilities

- Get to know the physician and how he or she likes to practice.

- Follow the physician for at least one day during regular office visits. This gives you an idea of the physician's style and also provides an opportunity to model effective ways to discuss GMAs with patients.
- Get to know all of the employees and physicians who practice in the same area as the GMA physician. Because this is a new visit type and can initially be viewed as threatening, it is reassuring for these people to know and trust someone who can answer their questions and concerns.
- Keep track of group appointment scheduling, and encourage the physician to keep the group census up.
- Show up at the GMA room 15 minutes early to be sure that the room is ready.
- Greet patients as they enter.
- Hand out name tags, releases, or any other documentation that patients need to complete before beginning the group.
- Start the group on time.
- Facilitate the group.
- Act as timekeeper so that everyone has an opportunity to address their issues and the group ends on time. Complete required documentation and review physician documentation for completion.
- Maintain regular contact with physician and staff outside of the group.
- Meet with the physician after each group for a few minutes to debrief.
- Be flexible. Anything can happen!

Nurse/Medical Assistant Role

Minimum Position Requirements

- Meet the requirements listed in the nurse or medical assistant job description.

Responsibilities

- Take the patient vital signs. Start 15 minutes before the scheduled beginning of the group, and complete after the group has started if necessary.
- Assist the physician with documents, lab slips, referral forms, and so forth, as needed.
- Participate in the group when appropriate and when time allows.
- Observe a group so that you have first-hand experience to use in speaking to patients.
- Be flexible. Anything can happen!

Scheduler Role

Minimum Position Requirements

- Same as scheduler job description.
- Excellent telephone skills.
- Ability to promote new patient visit type.

Responsibilities

- Schedule patients as the physician requested.
- Schedule patients as they call in.
- Offer the GMA to patients who want to ask their doctor a question or receive a callback.
- Offer the GMA to patients who are having a difficult time getting on the schedule in a timely manner.
- Visit a group so that you have first-hand experience to use in speaking with patients.
- Track the numbers of participants signed up for each group, and assist the physician and medical assistant in keeping the numbers up.
- Be flexible. Anything can happen!

This is not to say that these positions need to be new hires, but instead, these descriptions work as a guideline to map out the duties, responsibilities, and roles. This information needs to be considered when deciding who in the practice will participate.

Start-Up Marketing

When people understand this new paradigm, they are usually enthusiastic about it, but GMAs are a new idea. They require some explanation and endorsement by people who others consider important. It is vital for the physician to provide leadership and work with the rest of the staff in recruiting patients for the group.

Your start-up market has two tiers. First, you need to market GMAs to your staff. After the staff members are on board, they can help you market to patients—but the first and most enthusiastic endorsement to both staff and patients needs to come from you.

Marketing to Staff

When your staff is convinced of the value of GMAs, everything gets a lot easier very quickly. If you do not get your staff on board, it is very difficult to have a successful GMA.

The best way to begin this process is with education. Meet with the staff to explain the nuts and bolts of GMAs and to reassure them that this is not just another managed care cost-saving initiative. Get their buy-in. They are on the front lines, alleviating the concerns of patients whose participation is voluntary.

Give the staff members tools to help them succeed in enrolling patients into the GMA. I give schedulers a script of persuasive statements to use, such as, "The doctor believes in the benefits of the group and would like you to try it once," and "most patients feel concerned the first time and then end up loving it." Encourage staff members to use the statements you give them and also to rephrase these statements into their own words when they feel comfortable doing so. This will be easier after they have been able to observe a group appointment.

Box 6.3 includes some examples.

Flyers and Posters

Medical groups often put flyers and posters in the offices. Encourage patients to consider making their next appointment in a GMA. Here is a sample of the information that appeared on the flyer (Figure 6.1).

Posters are important because they are generally the first marketing tool that patients see regarding GMAs. Some medical groups elect to put a very generic poster in the waiting room and then others that contain more specific information in the exam rooms. If cost is a concern, having one poster in the waiting room will go a long way (Figure 6.2).

Marketing to Patients

Scripts and flyers are useful, but they alone cannot do the job. *Most patients come to their first GMA because of an interaction with the doctor or the staff.*

At first, you will have to reach out to patients. Do not assume that they will respond to a letter or flyer. You may need to call people and enroll them personally. After the word gets around and people discover how much they like GMAs, you will not have to do this. At first, however, set a goal for the census you want in the GMA. Then work as a team to make sure that you make your goal.

We found it useful to give patients a letter from the physician describing their excitement and plan for the use of the GMA when patients check in for their individual appointment. A sample letter is in Box 6.4.

Dr. _______ Weekly Family Practice GMA

(Group Medical Appointment)

OPEN ONLY TO DR. ________PATIENTS AND THEIR LOVED ONES

MEDICAL CARE, INFORMATION AND SUPPORT

Bring your questions, concerns and medical issues for discussion. Come any week you like and spend 90 minutes – 2 hours with Dr. _______and some of his other patients dealing with similar issues. This is an opportunity to experience an exciting new type of medical appointment in a warm and supportive group setting. Medical questions will be answered, prescriptions will be changed and refilled, medical tests and procedures will be ordered and test results discussed. Brief private examinations and discussions are available if necessary.

You are not alone. Be with others who can really understand!

When: ____________________________________

Where: Register at Dr_______ office 15 minutes prior to the start of your appointment, then proceed to the meeting room.

Cost: The co-pay is the same as for a regular office visit. Support person or spouse is free.

TO MAKE AN APPOINTMENT OR FOR QUESTIONS, CALL

(__)______________

The focus of this group is upon helping you MAKE YOUR LIFE BETTER.

Figure 6.1 *GMA Flyer Source:* **Sutter Medical Foundation, Sacramento, CA**

Marketing to patients is an ongoing process that we discuss in Chapter 8. When you have prepared yourself, your administration, your staff, and your patients, you are ready to launch your GMA!

BOX 6.3 HOW TO SPEAK ABOUT GMAS

(What is a group appointment? I've never heard of such a thing!)

- "It's a medical appointment where Dr ______ meets with a group of her patients for 60 to 90 minutes. It's a great opportunity for patients to spend more time with Dr _____ and also gain a wealth of helpful information from the doctor and from other patients that may pertain to your care. It is relaxed and interactive. All your medical concerns can be addressed (treatment options discussed, prescriptions written, labs ordered, referrals made, etc.). Often patients are reluctant at first to attend but the majority like them very much and find much benefit in them."

- "Dr ____ is excited about this and would like you to try it once and see if it is beneficial and interesting for you."
- "Often other patients have similar experiences to what you are going through and have helpful ideas. Also, you probably have something of value from your experience that would be very helpful to others."
- "Other patients often ask questions that may pertain to you, but that you might not have thought of asking. You may learn about health issues relevant to a family member, if not to yourself."
- "These groups have become very popular. Our patients tell us how much it helped them. The physicians love doing them, too."
- "If needed, you can ask for an individual time with the doctor at the end of the group."
- "If time is a problem, let Dr___ know and your issues will be dealt with first. If you need to leave and return to work, that's fine."
- "During this group, Dr____ prescribes, changes, and refills medications, goes over lab or test results, can follow-up from another appointment, answer questions, reevaluate treatment choices, etc."
- "Dr _____ can spend more time talking in depth about relevant health issues, and do more education."
- "You are very welcome to bring a spouse or support person at no charge."
- "Dr _______ is doing this because s/he wants more time with her/his patients, and the group gives everyone the opportunity to be more creative in health care."
- "Dr _______'s GMA is a tool for both the doctor and his/her patients. At times the doctor will ask to see you in the group, and at other times the doctor will ask to see you privately. But it's the patient's choice."
- "Dr ________ believes in the benefits of the group and would like each patient to try it once."

Source: © DeeAnn Schmucker 2006

BOX 6.4 GMA INFORMATION LETTER

Dear Valued Patient,

I would like to encourage you to take the opportunity to attend a new group medical visit program I am starting that is open only to patients from my practice. My Group Medical Appointment provides you with an extended 90-minute medical appointment. This group includes other patients from my practice (other professional) and me.

I am very excited about this new program, which will give us time to get better acquainted and to discuss your questions and concerns in more detail. This group also will provide you with support and information from other patients having similar experiences that can help you to better cope with your situation and live life fully despite health problems. During each group visit, I will be able to answer questions, prescribe and refill medications, order tests and procedures, discuss test results, talk about side effects and treatment options, and provide brief private exams when appropriate. These group medical visits are very informative, interesting, and more relaxed than a regular private office visit. Group medical appointments are meant as an additional option, not a replacement for individual appointments. There will be times when you will require individual appointments.

My Group Medical Appointment is available to you every _______ from _____. Please register 15 minutes before the start of the group, where you will pay your regular co-pay and we will then meet in the Group room.

Pre-register for the group by calling (___) ___-____ to make an appointment for the session you would like to attend. Please feel free to bring your spouse or another support person, as they will likely find the interaction helpful as well.

It is a pleasure to be able to strongly recommend this new program to you. It promises to be a warm, supportive, and rewarding experience. I look forward to participating in this group opportunity with you. For questions about this program please _______________ at (___) ___-____.

Warmly,

Source: **Sutter Medical Foundation, Sacramento, CA**

Chapter 7

Launch and Execution: The Nuts and Bolts

Welcome to your first group medical appointment (GMA)! Now what? This chapter takes you through the actual appointment and deals with the nuts and bolts of issues such as confidentiality, billing, Health Insurance Portability and Accountability Act (HIPAA), forms, and physical facilities.

Your Group Room: What You Need

Some groups and practices have an ideal room right on the premises, one that seems just to be waiting for a GMA! Other groups need to hunt a little to find appropriate space. Most office spaces are designed around the individual appointment. Some upfront costs may be involved in renting or remodeling a room to accommodate the group, or you may be able to convert space that is usually used for other purposes.

The optimal GMA room is one that seats about 20 people in a semicircle of movable, comfortable chairs. It would be near the area where the physician has individual appointments to let patients know that this is part of the practice and for convenience. It would also have a private exam room and a restroom near the main room. Lighting would be natural but would not shine directly in patients' eyes or make the room uncomfortably warm. The room must be easy for patients to access and have good ventilation, a sink, and a table by the door where patients could check in and make their co-payments.

DOI: 10.4324/9781003673521-9

The room would have educational materials, various health education models, information about education classes, and community resources. A whiteboard would be available for the physician and facilitator to use to illustrate how medications work, what is happening in the body with certain disease states, or whatever it is that the provider or facilitator wants to put up. Some of my facilitators would put up an inspirational saying or quote to start the group off on a positive thought. It is also important to have a clock on the wall opposite where the physician and facilitator sit so that they do not have to look at their watches. Cabinet space would also be available to store forms, pens, name tags, and so forth.

When a dedicated room for the GMA is not available, get creative with conference rooms or classrooms. The downside is that conference rooms are rarely near the area where physicians normally hold appointments and that they usually have large, heavy furniture that is difficult to move. This reduces the flexibility of the space. Advanced scheduling of conference rooms and classrooms that are in high demand will be important.

Break rooms and waiting rooms have also been used for GMAs, but this can be disruptive. Employees can either come in while the group is in session or cannot use the room for 90 minutes. Another problem with break rooms is that they are sometimes not very clean. Seating people in these rooms comfortably may require moving existing furniture.

Waiting rooms can actually be very effective for physicians in private practice or in a small practice. If the physician doing the groups shares office space with partners, the groups can be held during off hours. Sometimes we have found that the patients for other physicians can check in at a nearby waiting room and then enter a back door for their individual appointments instead of going through the waiting room.

Although ideal space is ideal, do not let the lack of an ideal space or the imperfection of available space stop you from having a GMA. I have been very surprised to find that the quality of space has very little to do with the patients' perception of their GMA. All of the patient satisfaction measures have been high regardless of the space. I think having adequate space, although good for the patients, is most important for the staff and functioning of the clinic. When space is inadequate, the staff and providers are the ones to make the concessions. It takes a lot of energy and planning to always convert rooms from waiting rooms, conference rooms, and break rooms into a treatment space for GMAs and then after the group again putting the space back into its original order, but it is energy well spent. The benefits of having the group for the patients are much greater than the effort to restructure the room. To deal with the space issue, some practices rent conference room space in the same building where the clinical office is located. Still, other practices have sectioned off areas in their waiting rooms with removable screens so that the space remains flexible.

Lois Northheimer, regional practice director for Sutter Medical Foundation, says, "Space is one of the first challenges in beginning group medical appointments. Under our current system, space planning for GMAs is generally not considered a good use of money." Getting space to do groups often requires much convincing and advocacy for the powers that be to put money into remodeling, if necessary.

Can you imagine if it was the other way around? What would happen if groups were what everyone was used to and a need was recognized to create space for individual appointments? How would we explain the financial benefit of taking space that can treat 12 patients and cutting it in half so that we could now treat 2 patients? Obviously, new space needs to be designed to give the rooms the ability to be flexible to appointment and education needs as they arise.

"Rooms for GMAs need to also be set up with clinical equipment, including plumbing for sinks," Lois Northheimer says. A new medical office building was recently constructed in her area, and much thought went into the rooms for GMAs. The rooms are located in the same clinical area as the practicing physicians who used GMAs as part of their regular practice. The group room has its own area for patients who are coming for the group to check in and pay any co-payment that is due. There is also a sink for the providers to use to wash their hands, and an examination room and a separate restroom are near the main group room. This is an ideal setting, but excellent care still comes from rooms without these items. It requires creativity to figure out how to deal with the obstacles that some rooms inherently have. Although it may take some time before a group room like this becomes the rule rather than the exception, it is important to keep this in your mind. When remodeling or moving to other locations is in the works, the idea of a group room can be considered along with the rest of the clinical needs.

Supplies

Most of the supplies that are needed for the group can be kept in a small area of the group room, if cabinet space allows or in a portable container. Be creative about how these supplies are presented in the room for the GMAs.

These are the supplies you will need for each group:

- *Name tags and fine-tip markers to write names.* Do not use pens. The physician needs to be able to see the names from anywhere in the room. Remember that patients write what they want to be called on their own name tags.

- *Clock.* Place the clock on the wall facing the physician and co-facilitator so that they do not need to look at their watches.
- Educational handouts as needed.
- *Physician's box.* This box contains anything that the physician might need during the visit: prescription pad, referral forms, and so forth.
- Pens and paper.
- *Action plan forms, if you decide to use them.*
- Confidentiality, HIPAA, and other forms.
- *Antibacterial dry hand washing agent, if a sink is not readily available.*

Pre-group Preparation

In order to have an excellent experience during the GMA, it is important that some pre-group tasks be completed, preferably the day before the group is scheduled to occur.

- Order the charts of those patients who are expected to attend.
- Review the chart to make sure that it has all of the latest up-to-date information, including labs or the results of other testing and notes from other providers.
- Sometimes the provider and/or facilitator finds it beneficial to review the chart before the group. This is especially important when the group is designed to include the provider seeing other patients that are on his or her panel.
- Notify or remind the patient of the upcoming GMA visit.
- Make sure that the physician's box is complete and up-to-date.

Before the Group Participants Arrive

- Make sure the room is clean and has adequate chairs for the number of expected patients and support persons. (Dirty tables are often a problem if you are using a conference room where lunch meetings are held.)
- Place all of the supplies such as action plan forms, confidentiality/HIPAA, name tags, and pens in an area in the room where patients can readily access them.
- Have a blood pressure cuff, scales, and other items needed for vitals in the space where vital signs will be taken.

Welcome to Your GMA!

You are all set. The day arrives for your first GMA. Patients have checked in as they normally would for an appointment and are shown into the group room. (If you want their vitals taken before the appointment, ask them to come early so they can do that first.)

At the time the appointment starts, you have 12 patients sitting in a circle, eager to participate in their first GMA. How do you begin?

The facilitator opens the appointment and sets the stage by introducing the new format and some important ground rules of the GMA. Although the co-facilitators will want to use their own words and, in time, will intuitively know the best way for them to provide pertinent information, the following sample script will give direction on how to create their own scripts. Box 7.1 shows an example of a facilitator introduction script.

Confidentiality

Confidentiality is addressed in three ways during GMAs. First, the patient is given the option of being called by whatever name he or she would like during the group and asked to make a name tag indicating that choice. It is imperative that the providers and other staff members use the name that the patient chooses. It is rare, however, at times, patients use a fictitious name on their name tag, and this choice needs to be honored.

The second time confidentiality is addressed is during the facilitator's introduction. Sometimes it is important for patients to discuss things that happen in the group with their families and friends. For example, they might share the experience of another patient to help explain or validate their own experience. This kind of sharing can help family members understand the patient better.

The third way that confidentiality is ensured is that each patient signs a confidentiality agreement stating that he or she will keep the identities of people in the group confidential. The confidentiality agreement says that they can share what happened, but not the identity of the person to whom it happened. As with all of the tools in this book, this form is used by many of my clients. A sample confidentiality agreement is shown in Box 7.2.

Everybody signs this form, including guests. Patients need to sign only this document during the first group. The facilitator reminds the group of its responsibility for confidentiality at the beginning of each session. In my experience of having thousands of patients in GMAs, only one time was confidentiality breached. This occurred in a small town, and the patient who spoke about another patient was asked to not return to the group—ever. This put the offending patient into a panic. We decided after a year of not allowing her in the group to allow her to return after having a private session with the facilitator about the restrictions of confidentiality. This happened four years ago, and another incident, to my knowledge, has not occurred. Generally, patients take the responsibility of keeping others' confidentiality very seriously.

BOX 7.1 FACILITATOR'S SCRIPT

Hello, my name is__________________ and welcome to Dr __________________'s Group Medical Appointment.

A group medical appointment is just like an individual medical appointment except here you will have the other patients in the group present while you speak with your physician. Another difference is that instead of waiting and having a few minutes with Dr __________, you will have 60/90 minutes of time. How many of you have thought of another question right after the physician leaves the room? One of the advantages of these groups is that you have more time and can ask those questions. Another advantage is the benefit of the wisdom of the rest of the group members. Many people here have had similar experiences and can help you find solutions. So we encourage an open forum and encourage you to share your personal experience with each other. Another advantage of Group Medical Appointments is that it occurs every _________ and you can use this as a tool to see your physician more often if you need.

We ask that you look over your list of questions and select your two biggest concerns to discuss today. Oftentimes, other patients will ask questions that may provide you with some of the answers you need, and if you still have questions, we will schedule you for another group until all of your concerns are addressed.

My job is to help Dr ___________ facilitate this group and part of that is keeping track of time. If I interrupt you, please know it has nothing to do with the quality of your statement, but my desire to keep things moving along.

I want to speak for a moment about confidentiality. You are going to hear stories in here that could be helpful for you to pass on to your friends and relatives. We ask that you only share the story and not the name or any identifying information about the person who shared their experience with the group. We will have confidentiality forms for you to sign before we begin.

Does anyone need to leave early? If so, we will take you early in the group.

Does anyone need to see Dr __________ privately? If so, we will save time at the end of the group.

The restrooms are located.

The coffee, tea, and water are.

Source: © **DeeAnn Schmucker 2006**

BOX 7.2 GROUP MEDICAL APPOINTMENT CONFIDENTIALITY AGREEMENT

Privacy is something everyone is concerned about when they come for group medical appointments. You have the right to expect that what is said here is private and confidential. Along with our commitment to maintain your privacy, you will also have a responsibility to respect and protect each other's privacy.

Please share useful information outside of the group, but what you hear and learn about individual group members should stay here.

Printed name____

Signature____

Date____________________________

Source: **Sutter Medical Foundation, Sacramento, CA**

Document the Visit

Physicians often have time during the GMA to complete their documentation while patients are talking with the behaviorist or with one another. A sample form for progress notes is shown in Box 7.3.

In some instances, providers or organizations like to develop templates to make charting the visit more efficient. Some providers prefer charting the note in the same fashion they use for all of their charting.

It is most effective and efficient for the provider to complete the documentation during the actual group. This takes some practice, but is very doable. The facilitator and the patients' use of the group to provide education and support free the physician to do the documentation. I often describe that the way that the facilitator and physician work is like a dance. The provider and facilitator take turns asking questions or providing information. The facilitator soon learns how to assist the physician with data collection in the visits. For example, while the patient is stating his or her reason for the visit, the facilitator can ask the patient some questions to clarify specifically what he or she hopes to achieve at this appointment. While the facilitator, group, and patient are interacting, the physician can use this time to review the chart for

BOX 7.3 PROGRESS NOTE FOR GROUP MEDICAL APPOINTMENT

Patient Name _____________ DOB ____________ MR#___________

Allergies to Drugs__________________ Medications

CC: ___________________ Name Dose Frequency

Hx of Illness ________ ________ ________

________ ________ ________

________ ________ ________

________ ________ ________

________ ________ ________

________ ________ ________

________ ________ ________

Vital Signs: Nurse_________ (Initials)

BP______ P______ T______ W_______

COUNSELING: (Time Spent) Etoh_____ Diet ______
Cholesterol______ Exercise ______ Diabetes______ Smoking_______
Other_________________

Assessment:

A____

B____

C____

Plan: ____

Pt to return; as needed

In _______ Days Weeks Months Group Individual

Signature_____________________ Date______________

Facilitator Signature____________________Date____________

Source: **Sutter Medical Foundation, Sacramento, CA**

recent lab work, health maintenance adherence, and documentation. This also gives the physician time to formulate questions.

When the physician speaks with the patient, this gives the facilitator time to observe the patient to see whether he or she appears to understand what the physician is saying. This is also a time for the facilitator to formulate some questions for the patient that have to do with potential risks in their living situation or other life stressors that could be directly adversely affecting their health.

I recommend documenting the visit as a GMA in the patient record. It clarifies for the provider the treatment options that have been used for each patient. Even though the facilitators' time cannot be billed, I recommend that the facilitator sign each chart. Both the documentation and billing need to be discussed with regard to internal policies and state and federal laws.

Billing

Billing for GMAs is just like billing for individual appointments, as the same CPT codes are used in the individual appointment. As in any appointment, a GMA must have the following data entered or collected for each patient:

- Vital signs and other routine data, charted as for any other visit.
- The clinicians participating in the visit must create a progress note—written, dictated, or electronic.

- An ICD-9 and CPT code for each patient service must be entered on an encounter form. The following CPT codes are generally used for follow-up appointments in GMAs: 99212, 99213, 99214, and sometimes 99215, depending on the level of service rendered. The 99213 code is used in about 90% of charges. This is a face-to-face visit, as described in the ICD-9 codes.

GMA visits should also be treated the same as regular office visits in terms of co-payments. Remember that just as in an individual appointment, the documentation or note for the group appointment must support the ICD-9 code used. In GMAs, the code used is determined by systems covered and discussion. The only real difference is that the decision about which code level to use cannot be based on time spent with the patient.

Physician groups that I have worked with generally use the same billing form that they use for other visit types. One of the main issues is that a set of group codes has not been developed for providers to use and may not ever be developed as the group visit still falls under the guidelines of the current codes. At this point, I am not aware of any insurance agency that has refused payment for group visits. This includes both government and private insurance providers.

With regard to billing GMAs, as in all medical appointments, the documentation in the medical record must reflect evidence supporting the level of billing. Each patient in GMA does receive a billing code that directly reflects both the chart note and the breadth and depth of the issues that were addressed for that individual during the group.

HIPAA

Many concerns have been raised about the issue of HIPAA compliance during GMAs. There are two answers to these concerns:

1. Anything that patients say or offer about themselves during the group is not of concern regarding HIPAA, as the patients themselves offer up the information.
2. Noncompliance with HIPAA becomes an issue only when the physician, provider, or a staff person shares information about a patient in front of the other patients. The sharing of information by the provider is done for a variety of reasons. First, physicians need to interact with patients in order to obtain data needed for discussion. They may need to ask questions or make statements that give information about the patient. Furthermore, physicians need to give information such as labs and other test results and to discuss those results with patients.

Because these discussions are not only necessary to provide an effective visit but also become excellent learning opportunities for other patients in the group, patients need to sign authorizations for medical disclosure during the

BOX 7.4 AUTHORIZATION FOR DISCLOSURE OF MEDICAL INFORMATION

One of the biggest benefits of group medical appointments is the opportunity to learn from other patients. This means you also have the opportunity to positively impact someone else's life. Knowing this:

I authorize __________ physicians to share medical information pertaining to my current medical issues with participants of a group medical appointment of which I am in attendance.

This authorization shall become effective immediately and shall remain in effect for one full calendar year from the date of signature.

I further understand that I have a right to receive a copy of this authorization upon my request.

Signature______________________________________

Date____

Source: **Sutter Medical Foundation, Sacramento, CA**

group process. This gives the physician and other staff members permission to interact with the patient as they need to in order to provide good treatment. It is important for each medical group doing GMAs to check with its own legal counsel to advise on the development of this document.

The language of the authorization for medical disclosure may be something similar to the one in Box 7.4, which was developed by attorneys and used at a northern California medical group.

For this group in California, patients must sign this form on an annual basis. It is always important to have your legal counsel review the document you use for authorization of disclosure to include the local and state laws in your area.

Ongoing Improvements

One of the great things about GMAs is that they are *yours*. You can tweak and adjust them to suit your and your patients' needs. GMAs are a source of constant discovery. Leave time after every group to debrief with staff to ensure that objectives are being met and to get or give feedback on various occurrences in the group. These discussions are not only a powerful training tool, but also help you fine-tune various aspects of the GMA.

In GMAs, physicians often discover things about patients that run counter to their old ideas. When they are open to seeing situations in new ways and to asking patients their preferences, they can take the care they provide to a whole new level.

For example, I was with a group of physicians who were fairly new to GMAs, and we were discussing what was and was not going well with their programs. One physician said that she loved her GMAs but did not like to see patients with diabetes in the group. This surprised the other physicians, as they were seeing patients with diabetes in their groups and found GMAs particularly beneficial for this group of patients. She said the problem was that after the group she had to put all of the patients in private rooms so that she could examine their feet.

The other physicians said they just examined their patients' feet in the group room, in front of everyone else, without any problems. She said, "My patients don't want their feet examined in public. *I* wouldn't want to take *my* shoes off in front of others." We discovered that her own discomfort led her to room the patients and check their feet without ever asking them whether they minded having their feet examined in the group. It is important to ask patients about their preferences and not to make assumptions about what they want.

GMAs give us the opportunity to discover the assumptions that we make daily about what patients want. In the group, you never assume what the patient wants but instead ask or state the following: "May I examine your eyes, nose, feet, arms?" "May I listen to your heart?" "Put down on your name tag what you want to be called." Instead of telling the patients what to do, what lifestyle change to make, or how often to exercise, ask them the following: "What are you willing to do to improve your health?" "How often can you do this?" "Will you come back to the group in 2 weeks and let us know how this change is going for you?"

I also run into many assumptions made by staff about who should attend the group and what is okay to be discussed in the group. One scheduler told me that "we need to be careful about having depressed patients come to the group because they should not have to talk about their depression in front of everyone. It would be too embarrassing." As both medical and mental health professionals know, one of the barriers to treating depression is society's general perception that depressed people are weak. Depressed patients often blame themselves for their depression instead of recognizing that this is a physical condition that requires attention from both medical and mental health professionals. What better way is there to break the stigma of shame over depression than to be able to discuss it with others and to find out the prevalence of it?

One of the things I have learned in doing GMAs is that patients are willing to discuss what we are willing to hear. I was working with a physician who told me her patients were reluctant to discuss their depression in her GMA. As I am a trained licensed clinical social worker, I was asked to be a facilitator in her group to check this out. During the group, I identified three patients who had significant depressions and one who I was concerned about the possibility of suicide and did a suicide assessment with her. During that assessment, the physician sat lower and lower in her chair. If there had been a hole in the floor to use as an escape, I have no doubt she would have used it. Every one of us has topics that we are not comfortable with. For some physicians, they are not comfortable speaking in front of a group with a patient about sexuality; for others, it is other items. I find that patients pick up on our cues and are often willing to discuss what we are willing to hear. When I facilitate a group, I hear very little from the patients about substance abuse. Does that mean that I happen to see patients without that issue? No, it means I need to look at my own comfort level about substance abuse and work to improve my approachability about that topic.

The previously mentioned physician discovered that she survived and that I, as the facilitator, but mostly the group, actually dealt with the issue. One of the benefits of the group is that the provider is not alone and does not have to be all things to all people.

Dr Janahn Scalapino, from Sutter Medical Group, Sacramento, California, has really described this well.

> It was with both anticipation and trepidation that I started seeing patients in small groups more than 2 years ago. What would happen if a patient made a scene about pain meds, seeing that others were getting prescriptions that she wasn't? What would happen if a patient broke down and sobbed? What would happen if I didn't have any good answers or suggestions for a particular problem and my ignorance would be broadcast to all of the participants? Each of those has happened, and with the help of the facilitator, the other patients in the group, and the patients themselves, problem solving has been taken to new heights. It is a thrill for me to see patients working together to comfort and problem solve, learning about conditions that they never knew about before. It's been a lot of fun and educational practicing medicine in the group medical appointment setting. It's a different approach to patient care, and I am learning how to be with an angry patient and a patient who is sobbing, how to deal with not knowing the answer, and how to communicate and be with my patients in a way that allows us to know each other differently.

Satisfaction Surveys

One of the best ways to make ongoing improvements is to stay current with patients and physicians about what does and does not work. This not only helps you adjust your program when and where necessary, but also becomes part of the evidence for success that fuels expanding your program. I recommend that patient satisfaction surveys are distributed and completed by the patients after every group for the first three months. These data will be extremely helpful as you fine-tune your group to best meet the patient and organizational needs. After that, patient satisfaction surveys can be completed as often as you like. A sample patient satisfaction survey is shown in Box 7.5.

Physician Satisfaction Survey

A sample physician satisfaction survey is shown in Box 7.6. For these surveys, I recommend that they be distributed and completed once every three months for the first year. After that, it is good to check satisfaction at least annually.

BOX 7.5 PATIENT SATISFACTION SURVEY

MD:
Date:

Have you ever attended a GMA?	**Yes**	**No**	*If yes, how many?* ______
Have you completed this survey before today?	**Yes**	**No**	

Thinking about this particular appointment, how would you rate the following:

		(Circle one number on each line.)				
		Excellent	**Very Good**	**Good**	**Fair**	**Poor**
1.	Availability of Appointment	**5**	**4**	**3**	**2**	**1**
2.	Courtesy and helpfulness of receptionists	**5**	**4**	**3**	**2**	**1**

3.	Courtesy and helpfulness of Healthcare professionals including Medical Assistants, Physicians, Nurse Practitioners or Behaviorists	**5**	**4**	**3**	**2**	**1**
4.	Time spent with the healthcare professional/s you saw	**5**	**4**	**3**	**2**	**1**
5.	Explanation of what was done for you	**5**	**4**	**3**	**2**	**1**
6.	Technical skills (thoroughness, carefulness, competence) of the person you saw	**5**	**4**	**3**	**2**	**1**
7.	The personal manner (courtesy, respect, sensitivity, friendliness) of the person you saw	**5**	**4**	**3**	**2**	**1**
8.	The visit overall	**5**	**4**	**3**	**2**	**1**
9.	In general, would you say your health is	**5**	**4**	**3**	**2**	**1**
10.	Would you recommend the group medical appointment to your family or friends?		**Definitely yes**	**Probably yes**	**Probably not**	**Definitely not**
			•	•	•	•

11. Are you (patient) male or female Male Female

Is there anything you particularly <u>liked</u> about today's appointment?

Is there anything you particularly <u>disliked</u> about today's appointment?

Thank You! We appreciate your feedback!

Source: **Sutter Medical Foundation, Sacramento, CA**

BOX 7.6 PHYSICIAN SATISFACTION SURVEY: GROUP MEDICAL APPOINTMENTS

Date:

Thinking about this particular appointment, how would you rate the following:

		(Circle one number on each line.)				
		Excellent	**Very Good**	**Good**	**Fair**	**Poor**
1	The quality of care this visit offers	5	4	3	2	1
2	Support from administration for this tool (space, co-facilitator…)	5	4	3	2	1
3	As a disease management tool	5	4	3	2	1
4	As a tool to assist with access problems	5	4	3	2	1
5	The ability to utilize your own creativity for treating patients	5	4	3	2	1
6	The effectiveness of GMA's in achieving your goals	5	4	3	2	1
7	The overall usefulness of this tool in your practice.	5	4	3	2	1

8. What did you initially want Group Medical Appointments to do for your practice?

9. What have Group Medical Appointments actually done for your practice?

10. Would you recommend Group Medical Appointments to your colleagues for their practices?

Thank You! We appreciate your feedback!

Source: © **DeeAnn Schmucker 2006**

Ongoing Success

To keep your GMA program successful and growing, you will need organizational support from all levels. Involve all front-line staff members early on in the success of the GMA. Solicit their ideas for ways to improve GMAs and make them run more smoothly. Buy-in from all levels, clear communication about goals, acknowledgment of everyone's contribution, and ongoing information about progress are crucial in further development of the groups in your medical practice.

One of the major mistakes I made early on in developing GMAs was that I only shared the satisfaction survey results with the facilitator, physician, and administration and did not share the results with the front-line staff. The schedulers, receptionists, and medical assistants, therefore, only saw the patients' initial reluctance to attend the GMA and not how much they enjoyed the appointment. After they saw the results, they felt more confident about enrolling patients in the group.

Be sure to keep administration up-to-date on the cost/benefit of the GMAs, collecting as much data as possible. This is especially important as you move from the pilot phase into expansion. We do this often for individual appointments, as that is currently the only tool that we have for seeing patients. Think of the resources we apply toward the evaluation and improvement of individual appointments. GMAs must have the same consideration. It is important for senior management to strategize how the GMAs fit into the daily operation of the medical group or practice.

Steering Committee

When you have four or more physicians doing GMAs, I recommend that you create a steering committee. GMAs are a new tool, and thus, it is important to have a regulating committee to make them a part of daily operations. The steering committee has the following functions:

- Set criteria on what makes a group successful.
- Allocate resources.
- Plan future GMAs.
- Decide on what outcomes to study.
- Allocate resources for education and training of physicians and staff for new GMAs.

I recommend that these people be members of the steering committee:

- Chief operating officer.
- Medical director.
- One or two physicians who are doing GMAs.
- Project manager for GMAs.
- One or two medical assistants or schedulers.
- Representative of quality management.
- Representative of information technology.
- Facilitator.

For the first year, I suggest that the steering committee meet every month. After that, they can meet quarterly. Again, one of the most vital functions of the steering committee is to plan and execute outcome and satisfaction studies. This not only keeps your GMAs in a state of constant improvement but also provides important evidence that they are effective when you want to initiate more of them.

The support, information, and decision-making that occur in the steering committee are valuable. Obviously, if you are in a private practice with just yourself or a few other physicians, the setup for a steering committee such as this is not feasible. If possible, however, it can be very beneficial to connect with other providers in your community who are also incorporating GMAs into their practices and have regular meetings to share information and discuss best practices.

One of the most important issues your steering committee will address is how to keep the census up in your GMAs (see Chapter 8).

Chapter 8

Ongoing Marketing: Keeping the Census Up

"But how do I keep the group medical appointments (GMAs) filled?" This is one of the most common concerns among people who are considering GMAs, and it is a valid question. GMAs do not fill themselves—at least, not at first. Until your patients begin to experience the advantages of GMAs and tell other patients about them, you will need to give the census some attention. The more vigilant you are about marketing GMAs in the initial stages, the better and faster they will fill—and the less energy they will require as time goes on.

Keeping up your GMA census is not difficult if you follow the suggestions in this chapter. These suggestions give you a four-pronged approach to keeping your GMA filled:

- Speaking about GMAs in a clear way.
- Marketing materials.
- Skillful scheduling.
- Physician enthusiasm.

Speaking About GMAs

The more clearly, enthusiastically, and forthrightly you and your staff speak about GMAs to patients, the more enticing they become. This is not always easy

DOI: 10.4324/9781003673521-10

because GMAs are a new idea. Some staff may be less sure about what they are and how they work than the patients are.

For this reason, all staff members should attend a GMA as soon as possible. They will be talking to patients who have no frame of reference for GMAs. It can be like trying to describe the color red to someone who has never seen it. To speak effectively and clearly and with genuine enthusiasm, staff members need to speak from personal experience.

One of the problems in communicating about GMAs is that sometimes patients have had negative experiences with other groups. They tend to believe that all groups will be like the groups in which they had the negative experience. They may make these comments: "I'm not a group person" or "I am an introvert" or "I have been to many support groups and am not in need of one now."

Staff members need to become skilled at explaining that GMAs are not support groups, that they are not like other groups that patients may have attended, and that people do not need to like groups in order to like GMAs. I usually recommend that staff members ask these patients whether they would be willing to try a group. Then they should give feedback so that the office workers know whether it was beneficial or what they could do to make it work better. In most cases, these patients end up loving the group.

What can you do to help your staff speak effectively about GMAs beyond letting them attend one and see the benefits firsthand? In addition to giving them the talking points about GMAs in Chapter 6, which answer the question "what is a GMA?" you can give them these "GMA answers," which are designed to answer specific patient concerns. You might even suggest that they keep these phrases by the phone so that they can refer to them. Box 8.1 shows potential questions and answers.

Keep the Benefits before the People

You might also give staff members a sheet of the benefits that patients report from GMAs so that they can refer to it when speaking with patients who are new to the group.

BOX 8.1 QUESTION AND ANSWER SCRIPT FOR GMA

(Patient expresses general concern or worry about the group.)

"I understand that you're concerned. Most patients initially feel concerned the first time, and they end up loving it."

(Patient says, "But I work…")

"We find that the group takes about the same amount of time as a regular medical appointment, if you include the time you might normally have to wait to see the doctor."

"We know that you're busy, and it's possible for people with a limited amount of time to go first if they request it."

(Patient is concerned about privacy.)

"If you have private concerns, ask at the beginning of the group to see Dr ______ privately at the end of the group."

(Patient asks, "What is this, a support group?")

"This is first and foremost a medical appointment. Because it's part of a group, there are opportunities for support and education. Often people who have a similar problem can give information that makes life easier."

(Patient says he or she has been to the group before, and prefers not to attend.)

"No problem, we will look forward to seeing you ________________ (date of individual appointment)."

These benefits would include the following:

- Patients can be seen earlier than if they tried to schedule an individual appointment. Appointments are available every week.
- They spend more time with the doctor and also benefit from the experience and questions of other patients—even those whose situations appear to be very different from theirs.
- Their emotional and psychosocial issues can be addressed, as well as their physical issues.
- They get the support of the group and are able to contribute to others.

These benefits should be reviewed regularly so that the staff members have them in their "bank" of things to say about GMAs.

Marketing Materials

Staff members should also be supported with marketing materials. These are physical reminders to patients that GMAs are available and beneficial. They might include the following:

1. *Letters.* Physicians should write a heartfelt letter to their patients about GMAs explaining what they are and how they benefit patients. I do not recommend mailing these letters. Not only is it expensive, but also people often do not take the time to read them at home. Instead, I recommend that the letter be given to patients when they check in for individual appointments. They can then read the letter while they are waiting for their appointment.
2. *Posters.* Brightly colored posters can be very helpful. You can list a few of the benefits of the GMA (such as "more time with your physician" or "partner with your physicians for better care" or "feel better now") on the poster under a positive heading. These posters can be placed in the waiting room and in exam rooms with the provider's name on them.
3. *Flyers.* Develop some nice stationery, and print flyers with some of the information on the poster as well as the details of the group: time, location, phone number for information, etc. In this way, you can change the information easily and often.
4. *Scripts.* This book contains several scripts for talking about GMAs. I have found that both scripts and role-playing can be very helpful for staff. You may want to develop your own scripts for situations not covered here, as needed.

How and in what order should you use these marketing materials? A good progression is this: Patients come to the office and check in. The receptionist gives them the letter that the physician has written. They sit down and start reading. When they look up, they see the posters on the wall. They go into the exam room and see another poster. The nurse then gives them a flyer with more specific information about the group. By the time the patients see the physician, they have already been exposed to the concept of GMAs four times and are better prepared to hear the physician's explanation and invitation.

Skillful Scheduling

The scheduler has an enormous impact on the success of GMAs. I have overheard schedulers tell patients this: "All I have left is the group." This puts the

GMA in a "second-best" position. Nobody wants to offer or accept "second-best" treatment—even though the group is far from second best.

It is important to remember that GMAs add opportunity—not only to be seen quickly or frequently, but also to receive "value-added" care with the presence of the co-facilitator and the support of other group members.

What Goes Wrong

Although patient satisfaction with groups is very high, these are some factors that can work against keeping the census up in GMAs:

1. It is a new experience, and patients can be reluctant to attend at first.
2. The physician forgets or is uncomfortable directing patients into the group.
3. Patients do not want to commit 90 minutes to the group and need to be reminded they can go first and leave if necessary.
4. Staff people have not experienced the group and are not convinced of its benefits; thus, they do not encourage patients to attend. Usually, after staff members have experienced a group, they are quickly convinced of the value.
5. Occasionally the group gets cast in the role of being second best or the last resort.

Beneficial Practices

These factors can be overcome very easily with a few beneficial practices:

1. During individual appointments, recommend the group to patients as follow-up, just as you would recommend a medication or other treatment.
2. Remind patients that this is a medical appointment, not a class or support group.
3. Direct patients to GMAs by saying very clearly, "I would like to see you in my group in _______ weeks. I believe I can provide the best treatment for you in that forum." You might also say, "I am doing these groups because I believe they will enhance my ability to have more time with my patients. Please try it once. If you do not like it, I need to know. I do not want to do this if it is not beneficial."
4. Do not select a few chosen patients for the group. Tell everyone about it. (A few exceptions to this rule are patients with memory disorders or patients who speak a language other than the one used in the group.)

5. Let patients who are already in the group help you encourage others. For example, if someone in the group has a successful exercise program, ask him or her to share how he or she got started and the benefits that he or she has realized. This will encourage new patients to continue.
6. Recommend this to your patients as the way you can treat them best. We do not invite patients to have sigmoidoscopies or other diagnostic tests. They still have the right to refuse. The same is true with the GMA. This is your tool. You need to decide whether the patient can best be served by following up in a GMA or an individual appointment. Both appointment types are valuable. We now need to be conscious of how we use them.

Purposeful Scheduling

The key to effective scheduling of GMAs is to be purposeful and intentional. Here are some examples of purposeful scheduling:

- During an individual appointment, the provider recommends that the patient be seen next in a GMA and asks the patient to schedule the GMA before he or she leaves the clinic.
- Schedulers offer the GMA first to patients before offering individual appointments.
- Letters are given to all patients as they check in.
- Physician, medical assistant, and scheduler all check to see that every patient leaves with a flyer about the group.
- The physician escorts willing patients to the scheduler in order to make the next appointment in a GMA before they leave the office.
- Queries on patient populations are run for specific disease management groups, creating lists of patients who have certain screening factors pertaining to a specific disease. These patients are then called and enrolled in the GMA.
- The physician looks over his or her schedule and asks that certain patients be called and asked to change their appointment from an office visit to a group visit. The script for such a call might be: “Hello, may I speak with __________? My name is ______________, and Dr ______________ asked that I call you and ask whether you are able to change your appointment from ____________ to his group medical appointment/GMA. The next group will be meeting ________ at ______________.”
- Patients are scheduled for their next GMA as they leave the group. This is especially beneficial when patients are attending the group for the first time. Even if the patient will not be attending the group for another month

or two, it is still important to put it on the schedule during that visit at which it was discussed. If patients go home without scheduling, they are less likely to be in the group. Two reasons are as follows:

1. They may have agreed with the physician to schedule a group but have second thoughts after a couple of days or weeks, and ask for an individual appointment when they actually call to make the appointment.
2. Some companies have centralized scheduling, and these schedulers are not always familiar with the groups. They may not be aware that the GMA is an option—thus, even when patients ask specifically for the group, the scheduler may not know anything about it. They are certainly less likely to advocate for the GMA.

Be sure that regular times are blocked out for GMAs as soon as the beginning date is set and that the scheduling template reflects the change indefinitely. Occasionally, times are blocked out for only a few months. The group will actually be going along fine, and then all of a sudden it does not happen.

It stops only because it no longer appears in the scheduling template! Medical groups that use centralized scheduling should make this template change ongoing so that the reception staff can schedule GMAs.

Keep groups scheduled ahead of time, but also leave some space for last minute patients. I recommend having the group three-fourths full one week before the date of that group.

We have found that the "no-show" rate in GMAs is similar to the "noshow" rate for individual appointments. After the groups get going and the patient population understands how they are used, the groups actually have a lower "no-show" rate than individual appointments. This usually occurs about a year after the group gets started.

Physician Enthusiasm

This may be the most important factor of all in GMA success. GMAs are successful if the following conditions are met:

1. *Physicians actively recruit patients for the group.* This means encouraging every patient to make his or her next appointment before leaving the group. It also means not just discussing GMAs, but recommending them.
2. *Physicians educate and inspire their staffs to advocate for this new tool.*
3. *This recruitment is very direct and explicit, and the physician uses phrases such as the following:*
   - "I recommend that you attend my GMA for your next appointment."

- "I am excited about this opportunity and would appreciate your feedback."
- "I would like my patients to each try this once to see whether this might work for them."
- "The best way for me to see you next, in order to provide optimal treatment, is in the group."
- "Many of my patients enjoy or benefit from the group."
- "It gives me more time to answer questions and provide information."
- "I think you have a lot to offer others in terms of speaking about how you have managed your chronic condition."

4. *Physicians and staff remain open to new ideas and concepts.*
5. *Physicians find a place for GMAs in their practice.* Successful physicians learn how to use this tool along with other tools in their practice to provide enhanced service for their patients. They see GMAs not as a substitute for individual visits, but as a more effective alternative.
6. *Physicians appreciate that this tool is the first real change in the patient–physician relationship in many years and that it requires the physician to educate patients, staff, and themselves on how best to use it.*

Dr Tuan Doan, from Sutter Medical Group in Rocklin, California, wrote the following about promoting GMAs in his practice. It echoes principles that I have found useful:

> Since beginning my group medical appointments in July 2001, I have been faced with an issue that all physicians face when they begin this type of appointment—how to promote and explain group medical appointments to my patients and staff. I have developed several ideas that have helped me to promote the groups.

It is vital to train the front staff on the benefits of the group and how you, as the physician, see the group fitting into your practice. Encourage them to offer the group first for follow-up appointments, especially for those patients with chronic conditions. Early on, my staff called patients and rescheduled office visits for group visits. After a year, my staff, patients, and I have a better understanding of how best to use groups, and rescheduling is no longer needed. Patients sometimes initiate the conversation about groups as they ask questions about them after viewing the posters and flyers.

Probably the most effective way to promote the groups is for me to explain this to my patients personally. I have found it is very important that patients understand that this is a medical appointment and that this modality is a way I have chosen to conduct my practice. Patients then feel they are still getting the best quality of care.

Most often my patients who have attended group report they are not the only one who has a particular experience, and I share this with patients who have yet to participate in group. Patients often relate to one or more participants of any given group and are able to learn about ways to take care of themselves through someone else's experience. Social support, whether it be for lifestyle changes such as beginning to exercise or changing the way they relate to others in their lives, is probably one of the more valuable experiences the group offers. When I describe some of those experiences to patients who have not yet attended, I find that they are more willing and often excited to try this new venue.

Summary

Group medical appointments (GMAs) are not only new but also revolutionary. They represent a major change in the patient–physician relationship. All changes take some time to assimilate. Patients, however, seem to grasp this concept much quicker than medical professionals. They are ready for this change.

Although patients are receptive to this change, some persuasion is initially necessary to enroll them into the group. Providers need to recommend the group to their patients just as they would recommend any other treatment option.

GMAs are not designed to replace the individual appointment. In fact, they enhance the ability for providers to treat patients by providing another tool for both providers and patients. Much of our time and energy in medicine is spent trying to make the individual appointment more cost-effective without reducing quality. Nothing is wrong with the individual appointment. The problem is that we currently use it as the only way to treat patients instead of creating other tools that are more effective. GMAs are one tool that takes some of the burden from the individual appointment and at the same time increases the quality of care, patient satisfaction, and physician satisfaction.

In order to have successful group appointments, three rules must be followed:

1. *GMAs are medical appointments!* They are not support groups, educational classes, or therapy groups, although support, education, and therapeutic experiences do happen in the group.
2. *GMAs are physician-driven.* Each provider needs to find a place in his or her practice for this tool, communicate that with others, and enroll his or her patients in the GMA.
3. *This tool is as large or small as your imagination.* For GMAs to be successful in a practice, a paradigm shift occurs from our current model of care to include other tools. We have yet to truly experience the boundaries of this tool, and clinicians are coming up with new ways for GMAs to benefit practices and patients. GMAs can be used in many different ways and greatly assist a provider's practice if the group is designed to address

pressing issues in that practice directly. As with anything, there are advantages and disadvantages to each type of group that need to be considered when planning the GMA.

GMAs can be done for a single practitioner or can be part of a larger disease management program. GMAs are excellent screening tools that can greatly assist the provider in helping the patient with lifestyle changes.

There are many benefits to GMAs for providers, patients, staff, and administration. Providers enjoy many aspects of GMAs. Here are a few examples:

- A more relaxed setting to treat patients.
- The opportunity to connect with patients and facilitate healing.
- Assistance in problem-solving from the facilitator and other patients.
- Being on time and not having to apologize for being late.

The staff enjoys the following:

- Not having as many frustrated patients to deal with on a daily basis.
- A scheduling slot to offer to patients when the provider's schedule is full.
- The opportunity to see patients get better.

Patients enjoy the following:

- The opportunities to learn from other patients, receive support, and contribute to someone else.
- More time with their provider.
- Better access, knowing that there is a flexible appointment opportunity for their use every week if they need it.
- Learning how to cope more effectively with chronic disease and how to enhance their quality of life.

Administration enjoys the following:

- High patient satisfaction scores.
- Happy providers.
- Better patient access.
- Providers' time leveraged by at least 200%

In order for GMAs to be most effective, support from senior administration as well as front-line staff is important. It is also important for everyone to observe a group or part of a group, as GMAs are not like any other types of groups. One of the best ways to understand GMAs is to see one in action.

A good way for administration involvement is to have a project manager who can manage resources, train providers and staff on how to do the groups, manage data collection, and report to senior management on a regular basis to keep everyone up-to-date. A GMA steering committee is vital for any medical practice that has three or more providers using GMAs. This committee is made up of a cross-section of senior management, providers, and front-line staff, and their primary task is to determine the guidelines for the organization's use of GMAs.

Besides the provider, other medical professionals may be used in the group appointments. Often someone is available to facilitate the group and a nurse to take vital signs. Sometimes others come to give educational information to patients or to fulfill other tasks in the group. All of this depends on how the group is designed.

Billing for GMAs is the same as an individual appointment. Bill for the level of service you provide. It is not what patients say in the group that is a concern of the Health Insurance Portability and Accountability Act (HIPAA), it is what the provider and staff say about the patient that can be a problem. Having the patient sign a form that gives authorization for treatment in the GMA can solve that issue. It is important, however, for each organization to go over this with its legal counsel and make its own decision on how this will be handled.

Because of the newness of this tool, consistent marketing must be done in order to educate everyone: patients, medical staff, professionals, and society at large. The vast majority of patients report that they enjoy attending the GMAs and soon learn how to use this tool to help them manage their own health.

GMAs can be one of the most exciting and rewarding aspects of any medical practice. I encourage you to experiment and to use your imagination to let GMAs give you solutions to your most pressing challenges.

If I can support you or if you have questions or stories about GMAs, please contact me at deeanns@surewest.net.

Be careful about reading health books. You may die of a misprint.

Mark Twain, U.S. humorist, novelist, short story author, and wit (1835–1910)

Frequently Asked Questions

1. Some of our physicians occasionally get some of their patients together and give them informational lectures on various topics. Are we doing GMAs?

   No, that is not a GMA and cannot be billed as one. A GMA is a medical appointment—not a class, a support group, or therapy group—even though education, support, and therapeutic interactions happen. The same components that are part of an individual appointment are also part of the GMA. The patient's vitals are taken, the chief complaint recorded, and medications reviewed all in a face-to-face interaction with a physician.

2. Can professionals other than physicians do GMAs?

   Yes, however, the service must be billable in the system with that professional seeing patients individually and billing for their services. For example, in most settings, midlevel professionals such as nurse practitioners and physician assistants bill for individual appointments and therefore can also bill for GMAs. The Veterans Administration, for example, has pharmacists see patients in a group appointment and bills the system for their time. Pharmacists also bill the Veterans Administration system for seeing patients in a GMA. It is important to remember that although the group may contain two or more billing professionals, only one can bill for the visit.

3. How do I bill and get reimbursed for GMAs?

   Most providers bill for a GMA in the same way using the same forms that they use to bill for other visits. The code used is based on the level of service provided to each patient in the group. In GMAs, services are billed on systems covered and decision-making but not on the amount of time spent.

4. How can I possibly give 12 patients a quality appointment in 90 minutes?

   One of the main ingredients that makes a GMA a rich experience for the patients is the interaction between the patients. We find that patients often listen better to the advice of others than to their physician. In a group, the physician deals specifically with diagnosis and prescriptions and encourages much of the health education portion to be discussed by the patients and facilitator. For example, if one of your patients is doing really well with exercising, ask the patient to share what he or she is doing, how he or she got started, and what keeps him or her going.

   The facilitator can also be instrumental in assisting the physician with some of the data collection by having the patient begin talking about his or her chief complaint and by giving that patient eye contact while the physician listens and looks through the patient's chart to get reacquainted with the current treatment plan for the patient.

   For those patients who come in with a long list, the facilitator in the beginning of the group asks them to pick their top two concerns to be addressed during the session. Often other patients ask questions during the group. If the patient still has more concerns, schedule him or her to come back regularly into a group until you have worked through his or her list of questions.

5. How do we make sure that we are compliant with HIPAA regulations when we see patients in a group?

   When patients are seen in a GMA, confidentiality is addressed in three ways. First, patients sign a waiver promising that they will keep the identity of all of the group members confidential. Second, patients wear name tags, and on these name tags, they write how they would like to be addressed. Most patients write just their first name; some use a fictitious name. It is generally harder to identify someone with only a first name than with a last name. Third, the facilitator discusses the importance of confidentiality at the start of every group.

Many providers use an "authorization for medical disclosure" document that the patient signs giving the provider and staff permission to discussion issues pertinent to the treatment of the patient in the group setting. Review any documents of this nature with legal counsel.

6. Are patients really willing to share personal information in a group?

Surprisingly, yes! In fact, we have found that patients actually share more personal information in a GMA than they do in individual appointments. I attribute that this happens for at least two reasons: first, patients have more time, and more topics are discussed in the GMA. Second, patients bring up situations that other patients contribute to, often sharing more and different information about situations affecting their health than they would think to discuss with their physician privately.

I find that medical professionals have by far the most difficult time with patients sharing information. We always think we understand the patients completely and know what they want. Remember that patients are offered an opportunity to share and have a choice of whether they share. Patients often choose to share.

7. What do I do with the patient that monopolizes the conversation?

We find that this does not happen often. Sometimes providers are reluctant to put patients that require a lot of attention or appear "needy" in a GMA for fear that they will take over the group. What we find is that these patients respond more appropriately in GMAs than they did in individual appointments because they have constant attention.

The facilitator's role is to redirect or even stop the monopolizing patient. Most of this can actually be taken care of at the beginning of the group during the facilitator's introduction. The part dealing with monopolizing may sound something like this: "We ask that you look at your list of concerns and pick your top two concerns or questions for us to discuss today. Often in GMAs other patients have similar concerns to yours, and generally, some of your other questions will be addressed during the group. We also recognize that there is a great deal of wisdom in this group, and we ask for you to share your experiences or thoughts, as this may help someone else. As the facilitator, it is my job to keep track of the time. If I interrupt what you are saying and indicate a need to move on, know that the interruption has nothing to do with the quality of what you are saying but a concern for time." This statement makes patients aware of time, and often they keep their comments brief. They also are aware of the facilitator, and if or when the facilitator indicates a need to move on, it is received well within the group.

8. What do I do when the patient requires a physical examination as part of the visit?

   Many of the physical examinations can be done in the group, thus presenting a great opportunity for educating the other patients. Generally, examining the extremities, ears, eyes, nose, and movement is easily accomplished in group. Some physicians listen to heart and lungs over the clothing; other physicians see the patients privately for that. Some providers have injections done in the group, whereas other providers take patients to individual treatment rooms for injections. Before examining any patient, it is important to ask them first if it is okay for you to examine them in the group setting. If the patient prefers to wait or the examination that is required is extensive and requires the patient to remove all clothing, then wait until the end of the group to examine this patient privately. Do not leave the room to do any examination during the group appointment, as it disrupts the group.

9. Do patients who attend GMAs all need to have the same condition?

   No, there are definite benefits to having a variety of conditions. In these settings patients learn many important things about their condition (such as that they are not alone, they do not have the worst disease, or they are not as bad off as they thought they were). No matter what the chronic condition is, lifestyle recommendations are all the same; they can learn coping skills from each other even though they may have different conditions.

10. What topics are safe to discuss in a GMA?

   Any topic the patients want to discuss is safe. Often patients are willing to discuss most everything, although providers may be uncomfortable. Topics such as sex, abuse, mental illness, and substance abuse may be discussed in group. Again, it is important for the patients to feel as though they have a choice. Some ways of initiating conversation about these types of topics (if the patients have not already brought them up) is to ask the following: "Is there anyone here who has taken an antidepressant," or "who has had or currently is having trouble with impotence or lack of desire for sex?"

11. What type of patient should I have come to my GMA?

Anyone you can get to come. Do not spend any time thinking about whether the person would like or benefit from a group. Offer it to the patients, have them try it, and let them decide whether this type of treatment is for them.

We have found that patients who have some type of dementia or do not understand the language that is spoken at the GMA; those who are severely hearing impaired do not get as much out of the group as other patients. I have had all of these and find that although the patient with dementia does not get much out of the group, the caregiver does. With the language difficulty, it is hard—not impossible—to have someone translating while the group is going on. In terms of the hearing impaired, as long as someone is there who can sign for them, the group is very effective.

Patients with psychotic disorders can also attend regular GMAs as long as they are not having a psychotic episode during the time of the group.

12. Is there a certain personality type of physician that does better than others in GMAs?

No! It is easy for physicians and administration to believe that in order to be successful with GMAs the provider needs to be outgoing or someone who enjoys conversing with others. What we have found is that the personality of the provider does not affect the success of the GMA. What does affect the outcome of GMAs is the providers' willingness to learn new behaviors and skills. They also need to have a vision of how this tool fits into their practice and actively recruit patients to attend the groups.

13. Will I need to hire extra staff to do GMAs?

    Generally not! This depends much on how you design your GMA and what resources you currently have available. The facilitator does not have to be a mental health provider, although there are benefits to this. If you have a small practice and desire a mental health professional to be the facilitator for your group, often physicians go to the community and hire someone on a per-group basis. Nurses and other allied health professionals also make good facilitators.

14. What do I do if patients give each other misleading information or make suggestions that I do not support during the group?

    This does not happen often, but when it does, it is a great educational opportunity. When patients offer information to one another that is not correct, providers can easily correct this with the right information. A way to deal with this may be to say the following: "I am so glad you brought this up; many people believe this to be true, and it is not. This__________ is the correct information." When said this way, patients are encouraged rather than discouraged to bring up this type of information, as they feel grateful for the correct information and also feel that they have contributed to the group. This also opens up the opportunity to give patients advice on how to get correct information within your system or websites you prefer on the Internet.

15. How do I complete the documentation?

    To take advantage of one of the benefits of group medical appointments, it is best to finish the documentation while in the group. This is where having a facilitator is especially helpful. The facilitator can lead a group discussion, provide health education information, or obtain psychosocial information about the patient while the provider is completing the documentation. The provider actually presents less in the group and relies on the facilitator and patients to do much of the problem-solving.

    Creating templates, especially for electronic medical records, can really assist the documentation process, requiring minimal work for the provider and an excellent note for the medical record.

16. How do I incorporate a GMA in my practice when I do not have time to do all of the tasks that I am currently responsible for?

    That initially feels like a catch-22 for most people. Although beginning group medicals requires some additional time and energy from the provider, GMAs help work down the backlog in a physician's practice, enabling them to catch up. GMAs often provide better access for patients. We have seen a reduction in phone calls, as patients feel more secure about being able to see their physician on a timely basis. Providers often feel like they are on a treadmill. Running faster and faster does not make the treadmill stop; it actually just makes the treadmill speed up and more difficult to stay on. In order to make changes, providers need to stop running, get off the treadmill, and try different approaches and tools.

17. Will patients get bored listening to me speak to each one of them in turn?

    Those of us who work in medicine often forget that patients have complete lives other than the disease or situation we treat them for. Even though the patient may not have or experience what the other patients are describing, often he or she has friends or family in similar situations. Patients report that it is very helpful for them to learn how to be a better support for those persons in their lives that have these issues. They also are excited to learn what they might be able to do with regard to lifestyle choices that can reduce their chances of having the particular disease or condition.

    I also believe there is an element of voyeurism. Just look at all the talk shows and reality television shows that are being played on our networks. These shows are very popular.

18. Is it asking too much of the working person to come into a group appointment for 90 minutes?

    Actually, people routinely spend about an average of 90 minutes when they see their physician privately. Time spent in the waiting room, exam room, and then with their physician really adds up. After patients learn how to used GMAs, we find that working people often spend far less time in the group than in the individual appointment. These people can come into the group, ask to have their issues discussed among some of the first patients, and then leave whenever they want. I have seen working people come into the group like this and sometimes leave early and sometimes stay for the whole group. They have better control over how their time is spent and greatly enjoy and appreciate this as they juggle their other commitments in their busy lives.

19. What happens if I make a mistake in the group?

    Some physicians worry that misunderstanding something or making a mistake in front of a group of patients will make them appear incompetent. In fact, what happens when a physician makes a mistake, which all will do in time, shows the group of patients that the physician is human. They generally think more highly of their provider when they see how the provider works to rectify the error and their confidence in the provider's ability increases.

20. How do I manage if someone has a serious health issue or breaks down and cries during the GMA?

    Often the other patients in the group are really the best help in these situations. When a patient receives a diagnosis in an individual appointment, he or she often goes away feeling alone, without hope, and overwhelmed with this information. This is when the group provides some of its best benefit for these patients. When this happens in the group, either someone has had a similar experience or knows someone who had a similar experience. The person who perhaps got some bad news is supported. The aloneness they feel is reduced, and there is a sense of hope when they leave the group.

    The reality is that the vast majority of what humans experience is not out of the realm of understanding for most people. Life is filled with more similarities than differences, and we increase isolation and despair as we place emphasis on the differences. So too with patients who have a difficult social situation, when tears appear, the other patients in the group offer support and appropriate community resources and linkages in the greater community to assist the patient with problem-solving.

Glossary: Group Medical Appointments

Action plan: This is a document that is used to plan specifically for actions that need to be taken in order to accomplish a stated goal or lifestyle change.

Al-Anon: This program is developed on the same 12-step principles as Alcoholic's Anonymous. It offers education and support to family and friends of alcoholics.

Attitude of abundance: This is a way of viewing situations in life in a positive light. Instead of not having enough, this philosophy looks at what you have and makes the most of it.

Baby Boomers: This term represents the people in the United States born between the years 1946 and 1964. These people are described as Baby Boomers because there was a sharp increase in the number of births.

Behavioral health: This term is often used in medical settings to describe mental health professionals, such as psychologists, social workers, and marriage and family therapists.

Behaviorist: This is another name for a mental health professional.

Catharsis: This is an experience or feeling of spiritual release and purification brought about by an intense emotional experience.

CHCC model: This term stands for Cooperative Health Care Clinic and is one of the first models of GMAs.

Coaching: This term is a specific set of skills or training that is used to help someone deal with problems and relationships and to set action steps toward solving those problems.

Condition-specific GMAs: These are GMAs in which patients need to have a common disease or set of symptoms to attend.

Cooperative Health Care Clinic (CHCC): This is a GMA model that has been well studied.

Corrective capitulation: This is a therapeutic occurrence discussed by Irvin Yalom regarding group therapy that helps patients surrender their old ideas or dysfunctional ways of doing things and adapting healthier, more effective responses from viewing the interactions of other people.

CPT code: This stands for current procedural terminology and describes medical or psychiatric procedures that physicians and other health providers have performed.

DIGMA: This is a group concept that Edward Noffsinger, PhD, developed. DIGMA stands for Drop-In GMAs. Although these say drop in, patients were requested to schedule appointments.

Disease-specific GMAs: These are GMAs for persons with the same disease, such as asthma, diabetes, and joint replacements.

Drop-In Group Medical Appointments (DIGMA): These are a type of GMA developed by Edward Noffsinger, PhD.

Existential factors: This is the recognition that we are essentially alone in this world. Although others can offer support and advice, we are responsible to choose when choice is available and accept the outcome when choice is not available.

Facilitator: This is someone who aids or assists in a process, especially by encouraging people to find their own solutions to problems or tasks. He or she organizes and provides structure for a meeting.

Glucometer: This is a small machine that measures the amount of sugar in the blood. People with diabetes use these to monitor blood sugar levels.

GMA: This stands for group medical appointment.

Health Insurance Portability and Accountability Act (HIPAA): This federal law makes a number of changes that have the goal of respecting and maintaining an individual's right to privacy.

HEDIS requirements: HEDIS is a set of standardized performance measures that are designed to ensure that purchasers and consumers have the information that they need to reliably compare the performance of managed health care plans. The performance measures in HEDIS are related to many significant public health issues such as cancer, heart disease, smoking, asthma, and diabetes. HEDIS also includes a standardized survey of consumers' experiences that evaluates plan performance in areas such as customer service, access to care, and claims processing. HEDIS is sponsored, supported, and maintained by NCQA (National Committee for Quality Assurance).

Heterogeneous model: This is a DIGMA that anyone can attend. Attendance is not specific to the diagnosis, but everyone present has the same physician.

HIPAA (Health Insurance Portability and Accountability Act): A federal law that makes a number of changes that has the goal of respecting and maintaining an individual's right to privacy.

Holistic medicine: This is medical care of the whole person considered as subject to personal and social as well as organic factors; "holistic medicine treats the mind as well as the body."

Homogeneous model: In this model of DIGMA, the patients all have the same disease or condition.

Hyperlipidemia: This is an increase in levels of triglyceride and cholesterol in the blood that can lead to heart and vascular (blood vessel) disease and/or pancreatitis (inflammation of the pancreas).

Installation of hope: This is a person's ability to see hope in what might seem like a hopeless situation.

Interpersonal learning: This concerns or involves relationships between people. People learn from each other, as experiences are shared.

Leveraging: This means making the most of the resources available.

Mind: –body component: This is the interrelatedness of the body. One part of the body does not get affected alone, but all parts experience to some degree the injury or disease.

Neurobehavioral tool: This is used to manage chronic pain and other chronic conditions using the interrelatedness of the body.

Paternalistic model of care: This is often a style of medical care used today in which the desire to help, advise, and protect may neglect individual choice and personal responsibility.

Physician-specific GMAs: This is a type of GMA in which the patient needs to be seeing the physician doing the group in order to attend.

Pneumonia vaccinations: This vaccination is given to people with chronic conditions, older persons, and others to prevent pneumonia.

Prenatal GMA: This type of GMA is focused on pregnant woman and is a way for women to get prenatal care, support, and information.

Primary care GMA: This type of GMA is held by a primary care physician in which only the physician's patients may attend.

Psychosomatic conditions: These relate to a disorder having physical symptoms but originating from mental or emotional causes. They relate to or are concerned with the influence of the mind on the body, especially with respect to disease.

Sansum pilot: This describes the initial GMA program set up by the Sansum Medical Group in Santa Barbara, California.

Soft costs: These are indirect, not direct, costs.

Steering committee: This group of people is selected to provide framework and guidance for a program or idea.

Sutter Medical Foundation: This is an affiliate of Sutter Health Systems in Sacramento, California, that manages the business aspects for several medical groups also affiliated with Sutter Health Systems.

Thought Control Class at the Boston Dispensary: J. H. Pratt developed this group in the early 1900s.

Triage: This is the process of prioritizing sick or injured people for treatment according to the seriousness of the condition or injury.

Visualization: This is a technique whereby somebody creates a vivid positive mental picture of something such as a desired outcome to a problem in order to promote a sense of well-being.

Bibliography

Beck, A., Scott, J., Williams, P., et al. (1997). A randomized trial of group outpatient visits for chronically ill older HMO members: The Cooperative Health Care Clinic. *Journal of the American Geriatric Society, 45*, 543–549.

Bloch, S., & Crouch, E. (2005). Therapeutic factors in group psychotherapy. *Columbia Encyclopedia* (6th ed.). New York: Columbia University Press.

Clancy, D., Cope, D., Magruder, K., Huang, P., Saiter, K., & Fields, A. (2003). Evaluating group visits in an uninsured or inadequately insured patient population with uncontrolled type 2 diabetes. *Diabetes Educator, 29*, 292–302.

Coleman, E., Eilestsen, T., Kramer, A., Magid, D., Beck, A., & Conner, D. (2001). Reducing emergency visits in older adults with chronic illness: A randomized, controlled trial of group visits. *Effective Clinical Practice, 4*, 49–57.

Columbia Encyclopedia (6th ed.). (2001–2005). New York: Columbia University Press.

Darves, B. (2003). Three doctors share innovative strategies for tackling common practice challenges. *ACP Observer, 23*, 5.

Hearon, S. (1984). *Group therapy* (pp. 2001–2004). New York: Columbia University Press.

Holman, H., & Lorig, K. (2000). Patients as partners in managing chronic disease: Partnership is a prerequisite for effective and efficient health care. *British Medical Journal, 320*, 526–527.

Lorig, K., & Holman, H. (1993). Arthritis self-management studies: A twelve-year review. *Health Education Quarterly, 20*, 17–28.

Lorig, K., Stewart, A., Ritter, P., et al. (1996). *Outcome measures for health education and other health care interventions.* Thousand Oaks, CA: Sage Publications.

Magid, D., Beck, A., & Conner, D. (2001). Reducing emergency visits in older adults with chronic illness: A randomized, controlled trial of group visits. *Effective Clinical Practice, 4*, 49–57.

Noffsinger, E. (1999a). Increasing quality care while reducing cost through drop-in group medical appointments (DIGMAs). *Group Practice Journal, 48*, 12–18.

Noffsinger, E. (1999b, June 19). *Providing "Dr. Welby care" through drop-in group medical appointments (DIGMAs).* Presented at the American Medical Group Association meeting, San Francisco, CA.

Noffsinger, E. (1999c, Fall). Will drop-in group medical appointments (DIGMAs) work in practice? *Permanente Journal, 3*.

Noffsinger, E., & Atkins, T. (2001, April). Assessing a group medical appointment program: A case study at Sutter Medical Foundation. *Group Practice Journal, 48,* 42–50.

Noffsinger, E., & Scott, J. (2000, Spring). Understanding today's group visit models. *Permanente Journal, 4*(2), 99–112.

Pratt, J. H. (1907). The class method of treating consumption in the homes of the poor. *Journal of the American Medical Association, 49,* 755–759.

Pratt, J. (1965). Trailblazer in group psychotherapy: An early experiment in groupnosis. *Journal of the American Society of Psychosomatic Dentistry Medicine, 12,* 14–20.

Reno Veterans Administration Hospital. (2004). Unpublished study.

Sadur, C. N., Moline, N., Costa, M., Michalik, D., Mendlowitz, D., & Roller, S. (1999). Diabetes management in a health maintenance organization. *Diabetes Care, 24,* 995–1000, 2001

Schmucker, D. (2005, September/October). Introduction to group medical appointments. *Journal of Medical Practice Management, 12*(2), 89–92.

Scott, J., & Robertson, B. (1996). Kaiser Colorado's Cooperative Health Care Clinic: A group approach to patient care. *Managed Care Quarterly, 4,* 41–45.

Scott, J., Gade, G., McKenzie, M., & Venohr, I. (1998). Cooperative health care clinics: A group approach to individual care. *Geriatrics, 53,* 68–81.

Scott, J., Conner, D., Venohr, I., Gade, G., McKenzie, M., Kramer, A., Bryant, L., Beck, A., et al. (2004). Effectiveness of a group outpatient visit model for chronically ill older health maintenance organization members: A 2-year randomized trial of the Cooperative Health Care Clinic. *Journal of the American Geriatrics Society, 52,* 1463–1470.

Sutter Medical Foundation. (2001). [A multi-faceted patient interactive visit model]. Unpublished study.

Sutter Medical Foundation. (2002). [Financial data]. Unpublished study.

Terry, K. (1997). Should doctors see patients in group session? *Medical Economics, 74,* 70–95.

Trento, M., Passera, P., Tomalino, M., et al. (2001). Group visits improve metabolic control in type 2 diabetes. *Diabetes Care, 24,* 995–1000.

Trento, M., Passera, P., Tomalino, M., Pagnozzi, F., Vaccari, P., Bajardi, M., et al. (1998). Therapeutic group education, I. The follow-up of patients with non-insulin treated, non insulin dependent diabetes mellitus. *Diabetes, Nutrition & Metabolism, 11,* 212–216.

Wagner, E. (2000). The role of patient care teams in chronic disease management. *British Medical Journal, 320,* 569–572.

World Health Organization. (1998). *Therapeutic patient education: Report of a WHO working group* (pp. 1–77). Copenhagen: Author.

Yalom, I. (1995). *The theory and practice of group psychotherapy.* New York: Basic Books.

Index

Made in the USA
Monee, IL
13 September 2026

63176212R00103